'DAT LITTLE NEW ORLEANS CREOLE COOKBOOK

BY CHEF REMY

A Certified Product Of Louisiana

RELCO PUBLISHING

COVER PHOTO: REMY LATERRADE
COVER DESIGN: REMY LATERRADE & SUSIE AYO
PAGE DESIGN: SUSIE AYO

© Copyright 1994 by

RELCO PUBLISHING

P.O. Box 3942
Lafayette, La 70502-3942

ISBN 0-9632197-2-3   "Library of Congress Catalog Card Number" 94-092209

CHEF REMY has published this cookbook in order to make available one of the styles of delicious Creole cuisine that can be prepared with familiar condiments and ingredients. Information on those ingredients that are not available in your area can be obtained by writing CHEF REMY at address listed above..

All recipes have been tested by the editor, but differences in meat types, oven and stove temperature, elevation, cooking utensils, and availability of necessary ingredients must be considered in all instances of success and failure. Every attempt has been made to keep the recipes simple, yet complete.

❧ DEDICATION ❧

THIS BOOK IS DEDICATED FIRST AND FOREMOST
TO OUR LORD JESUS CHRIST
WITH WHOM ALL THINGS ARE POSSIBLE.

IT IS ALSO DEDICATED
TO THE PEOPLE OF SOUTH LOUISIANA.

'DAT LITTLE NEW ORLEANS CREOLE COOKBOOK

Because of the great demand for Louisiana recipes I have decided to provide this series of more specialized and compact versions of the traditional cookbook: "The Mini cookbook".

This cookbook contains a variety of recipes from the many ethnic groups that inhabit the New Orleans area. They will naturally be Creole recipes since that influence is depicted as the focus of historical facts given. I, however come from a French/Italian background and some recipes will reflect that heritage. Make no mistake, this is a New Orleans cookbook. As you flip through this book you will find there are plenty of recipes to cook in an easy to follow format. Don't be surprised at the size because as we all know...good things come in small packages.

(CONTINUES)

Cajun is certainly a part of south Louisiana cooking. It is true that many people associate Cajun with New Orleans. While it has become an integral part of New Orleans cooking, the main focus of this cookbook will be on the more traditional styles of New Orleans cooking as reflected by the many original influences i.e., Creole, Spanish, French and Italian. I do, however, want to provide as much information as space will allow, so here are some definitions that will help you with your Louisiana experience.

✑ ABOUT THE AUTHOR ✑

Chef Remy was born, raised in, and is a current resident of south Louisiana. His cooking experience goes back to age 9 when he first took an interest in cooking. His mother is a great cook of Italian heritage and would spend hours preparing the daily offerings.

He began to get serious about cooking when he was just out of high school, but was not able to go into the field until much later in life. While living among the Cajun people in Lafourche parish he began to write his first cookbook called, "I WANT 'DAT CAJUN COOKBOOK". He has since been able to pursue his dream of cooking professionally while cooking in and managing a restaurant. He has also cooked in two other restaurants, while cooking and coordinating for two catering services. Chef Remy enjoys cooking at festivals and gift shows whenever possible. He was named "Grand Champion" of the Ville Platte, La. Smoked Meat Festival in June of 1993. His commitment to continued education and

(CONTINUES)

excellence has placed him among the truly committed Louisiana cooks.

"Raising your level of cooking in the Louisiana professional cooking community is so important because of the fierce competition and because of the level of quality cuisine that has been achieved here. The standards of cooking in the world are being set in south Louisiana and to be learning and working here is truly an honor", says Chef Remy.

His cooking comes from the heart, which is an attitude that exists in the Cajun lifestyle. His desire to share his recipes with you is culminated in this series of mini-cookbooks. If you are a collector, then these books are great to make a part of your collection. If you just like to cook, then you must certainly add the passion of Cajun cooking to your repertoire.

❧ About Growing up in New Orleans ❧

Everyone's memories are rooted somewhere, mine are in New Orleans. I grew up in the 9th ward area of the great city. From that area came what is commonly known as "Yats". The most popular greeting in the city was "Where Y'at?". The dialect is lazy and has a personality that is totally unique to New Orleans. This uneducated sounding speech has been compared to the Bronx in New York. While there are similarities to this laziness of this dialect, that is where it ends.

Values were very important as a child growing up in New Orleans. Neighborhoods were very important as well. Everyone knew everyone else, and in a pinch could, depend on each other to watch out for the community's well being. We lived near the river, so the sounds of ships and trains changing cars became something to sleep by. Living and growing up in New

8

(Continues)

Orleans shielded me from the great differences of the town in relation to other Louisiana towns, or even any town in the world. New Orleans is truly a unique experience. The movies get close, but to truly feel it you must visit this great city.

Food is always a part of any American culture. It seems that in New Orleans food, along with music is the culture. I have been cooking since I could reach the stove, and look at cooking as an art form. It is the only art form that can appeal to all the senses. You actually get to eat the finished art. If you purchased this cookbook in New Orleans, or ordered it, or got it from a friend you will be able to enjoy a part of what New Orleans has to offer. It is said that people eat to live but in New Orleans we live to eat. So eat hearty.

✑ TERMS TO UNDERSTAND ✑

BISQUE   Is a thick spicy soup, usually with a cream base and some meat or seafood.

BLACKENED   To fry a season-coated piece of meat or fish in butter on a very high temperature until black in color.

CAJUN TRINITY   Chopped onion, bell pepper and celery.

CARAMELIZE   To saute' onion, bell pepper and celery in butter until moisture is gone and vegetables begin to brown.

(CONTINUES)

ETOUFFEE'   To "etouffee" is to smother with onions and other vegetables (Usually bell pepper and celery).

FRICASSEE   To cook meat or fowl in butter and then in a seasoned liquid.

GRILLADE   Thinly sliced strips of meat (usually pork) that are pan fried.

GUMBO   Basically a Cajun soup that has a roux base.

JAMBALAYA   Everything mixed together and cooked in one pot, with rice and stock, and cooked until rice has absorbed almost all liquid.

PANNE'   To fry a breaded or floured meat in a small amount of oil on high heat. This is usually done in a cast iron skillet, but any skillet will do.

11

(CONTINUES)

REDUCE
To bring to a boil, and through evaporation reduce the amount of water to concentrate the essences in a less diluted mixture.

ROULADE
Rolled meat or poultry.

ROUX
Roux is simply a mixture of oil or butter and flour. There are three basic rouxs for cooking. The white roux which is used in white sauces and for simple thickening. The tight (or medium roux) is a paper bag colored mixture used for thickening and flavor. Finally there is a dark roux that is used primarily for color and flavor. (Instructions to follow)

STOCK
Water that has been enriched by boiling parts of meat and/or vegetables until the essence of the parts has become a part of the liquid. Always strain stocks and skim fat to assure a pure and lo-cal source of flavor and nutrition.

(CONTINUES)

∽ Cajun Meats ∾

ANDOUILLE   Usually a large diameter sausage that is made up of pork and seasoning that is smoked until completely cooked. Used in gumbos and jambalayas.

SMOKED SAUSAGE   Cajun smoked sausage is similar to most smoked sausages except that it is usually more highly seasoned and smoked with a variety of wood from hickory to pecan or oak.

TASSO   Tasso is a very lean, thinly sliced pork that is highly seasoned and smoked to perfection. Tasso can be used as a meat source or as a type of seasoning to enhance vegetables or sauces.

✒ THE ROUX ✒

WHITE ROUX   The white roux is simply butter or margarine and flour. This is the base of white sauces, cream sauces and white or sawmill gravy. It is made by melting butter and adding flour and blending completely. In this case there is usually more butter than flour. I recommend for every tablespoon (15ML) of butter you add 1½ tablespoons (23ML) of flour.

TIGHT ROUX   The tight (light brown or medium) roux is used primarily to thicken, although it is flavorful as well. This is made with either butter or oil and flour (although I recommend butter). Equal parts of butter and flour are used to achieve this roux. Melt butter (or heat oil) and add flour. Whisk together and continue on medium high heat until mixture thickens and becomes a paper bag brown color.

14

(CONTINUES)

DARK ROUX   The dark roux is possibly the most used roux in Creole/Cajun cooking. There are several opinions about the color of a dark roux. I use a very dark colored roux (about the color of dark chocolate) and have a definite style of preparing it. Most say to mix equal amounts of oil (do not use butter, use an oil that can stand up to high heat, i.e. peanut oil or canola), and flour, but as you become familiar with the process I suggest you increase the flour by about 20%.

HOW TO COMPLETE THE DARK ROUX

It is essential that you understand the importance of a successfully completed roux. Since it is an integral part of many Creole/Cajun recipes you must not scorch or burn the roux. When you first begin to make a roux you will experience a very distinctive smell. In fact, the completed roux will have a slightly burned flour smell. If you follow the instructions to the letter you will not burn the roux. You must use patience in this process. If you are not

(CONTINUES)

patient you will surely burn the roux or will not achieve the desired color. Once you have mastered the process, this smell will become pleasant to you and all in your household, because the smell means something good is coming from the kitchen.

Heat oil to slightly hot. Add flour and blend with the utensil of your choice (most people say a wooden spoon, some use a metal spatula, I use a wire whisk). YOU MUST WHISK OR STIR THE MIXTURE, CONSTANTLY SCRAPING THE BOTTOM AND EDGES UNTIL ROUX IS COMPLETED! Keep on high heat until flour begins to brown. When the oil begins to smoke you must reduce heat to medium or medium high (depending on your skill) and continue to whisk or stir until the roux gets to a dark brown color. At this stage you can do a couple of things. You can remove the roux from heat and stir until the roux is cool enough to stop darkening. If you choose this process you must remove

16

the roux before you reach the desired color. It will progress to a darker color because of the heat that is retained in the oil. The other option is to remove from heat when the roux is almost the color you want and add chopped fresh onion to the hot roux and stir until the onions stop steaming. (CAUTION! THE STEAM FROM THE ONIONS WILL BURN YOU IF YOU ARE NOT CAREFUL). I use the latter method.

∽ RECIPE TO MAKE DUE ∾

1ST HAVE COMPLETE FAITH IN GOD TO PROVIDE ALL YOUR NEEDS

2ND SEPARATE THE THINGS YOU WANT FROM THE THINGS YOU NEED

3RD APPRECIATE ALL THAT YOU HAVE

4TH NEVER BE JEALOUS OF WHAT OTHERS HAVE

5TH SHARE WHAT YOU HAVE WITH THOSE LESS FORTUNATE

6TH KEEP A POSITIVE OUTLOOK

Mix all ingredients with love and compassion. Fold in Kindness to Eliminate bitterness and serve in large portions. This recipe is not fattening and can be used in any amount. Recommended for morning use, but can be used all day long.

POSSIBLE SIDE EFFECTS:
CONTENTMENT • HAPPINESS • A LOT OF SMILING • LOTS OF FRIENDS

✍ Appetizer's ✍

Food Quantities for 25 servings

Rolls	4 doz
Bread	50 slices or 3 1 lb. loaves
Butter	½ lb
Mayonnaise	1 cup
Mixed Filling for Sandwiches	
meat, eggs, fish	1½ quarts
Mixed Filling, Sweet, fruit	1 quart
Jams & Preserves	1½ lb
Crackers	1½ lb
Cheese (2 oz. per serving)	3 lb
Soup	1½ gal
Salad Dressings	1 pt
Potato Salad	4½ quarts
Scalloped Potatoes	4½ quarts or 1-12x20" pan
Mashed Potatoes	9 lb
Spaghetti	1¼ gal
Baked Beans	¾ gal
Jello Salad	¾ gallon
Canned Vegetables	1 #10 can
Lettuce (for salads)	4 heads
Carrots, 3 oz. or ½ cup	6¼ lb
tomatoes	3-5 lb
Wieners, beef	6½ lbs
Hamburger	9 lbs
Turkey or Chicken	13 lbs
Fish, large, whole	13 lbs
Fish, filets or steaks	7½ lbs
Watermelon	37½ lbs
Fruit Cup (½ cup per serving)	3 quart
Cake	1-10x12 sheet cake
	1½ 10" layer cake
Ice Cream, Brick	3¼ quarts
Bulk	2¼ quarts
Coffee	½ lb and 1½ gal. water
Tea	1/12 lb and 1½ gal. water
Lemonade	10 to 15 lemons, 1½ gal. water

∽ COCKTAIL SAUCE ∽

THIS IS A GOOD SAUCE TO HAVE WITH ANY SEAFOOD YOU EAT, BOILED OR FRIED. BUT AS A SPECIAL SAUCE, AS ANY SPECIAL SAUCE, YOU WILL FIND THAT IT WORKS WELL WITH VEGIES, MEATS OR AS A TOPPING FOR SEAFOOD SALADS. EXPERIMENT, AND FIND HOW YOU LIKE IT BEST.

1 CUP (250ML)	KETCHUP	3 TBSP (45ML)	FRESH PARSLEY, MINCED
2 TBSP (30ML)	HORSERADISH	2 TBSP (30ML)	WORCESTERSHIRE SAUCE
2 TSP (10ML)	LEMON JUICE		SALT AND PEPPER TO TASTE
¼ CUP (63ML)	SWEET RELISH	10 DROPS	TABASCO BRAND
3 TBSP (45ML)	GARLIC, MINCED		PEPPER SAUCE

Mix all ingredients together. Chill at least 2-4 hours. Have plenty for a seafood boil, it goes fast.

✂ CHEESE AND SHRIMP STUFFED MUSHROOMS ✂

THE GREAT THING ABOUT STUFFING IS THAT YOU CAN BE AS CREATIVE AS YOU WISH. THE COMBINATION OF CHEESE AND SHRIMP IS DEFINITELY A GOOD ONE. IN YOUR NOTES OF THIS RECIPE, I SUGGEST YOU KEEP TRACK OF THE VARIATIONS YOU COME UP WITH. MAYBE YOU CAN ADD SOME CRABMEAT, HAM OR SAUSAGE OR REALLY ANYTHING THAT YOU FEEL WILL ADD TO THE TASTE OF THIS GREAT APPETIZER OR ENTREE'.

1 LB (450G)	FRESH MUSHROOMS, LARGE	4 OZ (113G)	AMERICAN CHEESE
¼ LB (113G)	BUTTER	4 OZ (113G)	MOZZARELLA CHEESE
½ CUP (125ML)	SHALLOTS, FINELY CHOPPED	1 CUP (250ML)	BREAD CRUMBS
½ CUP (125ML)	MILK OR CREAM PREFERRED	1 LB (450G)	SHRIMP, PEELED, CHOPPED,
1 TBSP (15ML)	ALL-PURPOSE FLOUR		COOKED AND DRAINED
4 OZ (113G)	SHARP CHEDDAR CHEESE	1 TBSP (15ML)	CREOLE SEASONING

20

(CONTINUES)

Clean mushrooms, pull stems and chop fine. Melt butter and add onion. Cook until color brightens. Add milk with flour mixed in and bring to bubble. Add cheeses, a little at time until mixed well. Note: Shredded cheeses will blend more easily and the mixture should be fairly thick. Add bread crumbs and mix well. Add shrimp, creole seasoning, mix well and cook 10-15 minutes on simmer, stirring frequently. Let cool, then generously fill mushroom caps with mixture. Cover and bake at 375°F (190°C) for 20 minutes. Check mushrooms for darkening to a dark brown color. Serve. Be cautious of hot cheese filling when you eat. Serves 6-8.

ɷ New Orleans Style Garlic Bread ɷ

2 TBSP (30ML)	OLIVE OIL
½ LB (225G)	BUTTER
¼ CUP (63ML)	GARLIC, MINCED
1 TBSP (15ML)	PARSLEY FLAKES
¼ CUP (63ML)	PARMESAN CHEESE
2	LOAVES FRENCH STYLE BREAD

In a small saucepan heat olive oil. Melt butter and add garlic and parsley flakes. Slice bread in half lengthwise. Coat both pieces on the inside and bake in a preheated 400°F (205°C) oven for 5-10 minutes until top begins to brown. Remove, sprinkle with parmesan cheese, slice and serve.

✆ DIP FOR RAW VEGETABLES ✆

THIS IS A GOOD TASTING VEGGIE DIP FOR THAT VEGETABLE TRAY THAT YOU PLACED AT THE END OF THE FOOD TABLE. DON'T BE SURPRISED WHEN EVERYONE MIGRATES TO THE END OF THE TABLE.

1 CUP (250ML)	MAYONNAISE
1 CUP (250ML)	SOUR CREAM
1 TSP (5ML)	TABASCO BRAND PEPPER SAUCE
1 TSP (5ML)	PARSLEY
1 TSP (5ML)	DILL WEED
¼ CUP (63ML)	RANCH DRESSING

Mix all ingredients and chill for one hour. Serve with raw vegies.

✑ CHICKEN STRIPS ✑

4	CHICKEN BREASTS
½ CUP (125ML)	BUTTERMILK
¼ CUP (63ML)	MAYONNAISE
¼ CUP (63ML)	RANCH STYLE DRESSING
¼ CUP (63ML)	ALL-PURPOSE FLOUR
1 TBSP (15ML)	CREOLE SEASONING
1 TSP (5ML)	SALT
2 CUPS (500ML)	CORN FLOUR
1 QUART (1 LITER)	OIL FOR FRYING

Pound the chicken breasts with a meat mallet to make thin. Placing chicken in a zip lock type clear plastic bag will help. Cut the chicken into strips about ⁵⁄₁₆" (15mm) square, cutting the longest possible strips. Refrigerate chicken until ready to use.

(CONTINUES)

In a 1 quart (1 liter) bowl, mix buttermilk, mayonnaise, ranch style dressing, all-purpose flour, creole seasoning and salt until completely blended. A wire whisk or food processor works well. In a 2 quart (2 liter) pot pre-heat the oil to 350°F (175°C).

Place chicken pieces into batter and mix in until completely coated. Put corn flour into a separate bowl. Pull out pieces of coated chicken allowing excess batter to drip off. Drop coated chicken into corn flour and coat completely. Carefully drop chicken into hot oil and fry until golden brown. Serve with french fries, honey mustard dressing or your favorite BBQ sauce.

❧ Hot Seafood Dip ❧

¼ LB (113G)	BUTTER	1 TSP (5ML)	ROSEMARY
½ CUP (125ML)	ONION, FINELY CHOPPED	1 LB (450G)	SHRIMP, 150-200 COUNT PEELED
¼ CUP (63ML)	CELERY, FINELY MINCED	3 TBSP (45ML)	ALL-PURPOSE FLOUR
3 TBSP (45ML)	GARLIC, FINELY MINCED	1 QUART (1 LITER)	HEAVY CREAM
2 TBSP (30ML)	PARSLEY, DRIED	1 LB (450G)	CREAM CHEESE
2 TBSP (30ML)	WHOLE SWEET BASIL	1 CUP (250ML)	VELVEETA, OR SOFT CHEDDAR,
1 TSP (5ML)	TABASCO BRAND		SWISS, AMERICAN BLEND
	PEPPER SAUCE	½ LB (225G)	CRAWFISH,
1 TSP (5ML)	SALT		COOKED AND PEELED
1 TSP (5ML)	CAYENNE PEPPER	½ LB (225G)	LUMP CRABMEAT,
1 TBSP (15ML)	WHOLE THYME		CLEANED OF ALL SHELL

26

(CONTINUES)

In a 6 quart (6 liter) pot melt butter on high heat. Add onion, celery, garlic, parsley, basil, TABASCO, salt, cayenne pepper, thyme, rosemary and saute' until onion begins to wilt (about 5 minutes). Next, add shrimp and cook until all are pink. Add all-purpose flour and mix well. Add heavy cream and stir well until all ingredients are blended. Bring to a rolling bubble, stirring frequently, cover and simmer for 10 minutes on very low heat. Stir well, then add cream cheese and velveeta broken up into small pieces. Stir until cheese is completely melted. Bring back to high heat and bring to a rolling bubble. Remove from heat and gently stir in crawfish and lump crabmeat. Cover and let stand for 15 minutes. Uncover and serve with heavy chips or crackers, or for a better presentation provide pastry shells for your guests to help themselves. Makes about 3 quarts (3 liters).

✧ Fried Mushrooms ✧

1 LB (450G)	SMALL MUSHROOMS	½ TSP (2.5ML)	GARLIC POWDER
2 CUPS (500ML)	ALL-PURPOSE FLOUR	1	EGG
1 CUP (250ML)	CORN FLOUR (FISH FRY)	¾ CUP (175ML)	EVAPORATED MILK
1 TSP (5ML)	SALT	2 TBSP (30ML)	CREOLE MUSTARD
1 TSP (5ML)	CAYENNE PEPPER	1 QUART (1 LITER)	OIL FOR FRYING

Wash mushrooms and set aside on a paper towel to dry. Mix all-purpose flour, corn flour, salt, cayenne pepper and garlic powder in a bowl. In another bowl, blend egg, milk and creole mustard until completely blended. Add ¼ cup (63ml) dry mixture to egg mixture and whisk until totally blended. Put oil on heat until approximately 350°F (175°C). When oil is hot, dip mushrooms into egg mixture and then into dry mixture. Shake excess & fry until brown.

✑ ARTICHOKE BALLS

2 CUPS (500ML)	MARINATED ARTICHOKE HEARTS
½ CUP (125ML)	ROMANO CHEESE, GRATED
1 TBSP (15ML)	GRANULATED GARLIC
1 TSP (5ML)	SALT
4	EGGS
¼ CUP (63ML)	OLIVE OIL
2-3 CUPS (500-750ML)	ITALIAN BREAD CRUMBS

Pre-heat oven to 375°F (185°C). Place all ingredients except bread crumbs into a food processor. Process until totally blended. Add bread crumbs until mixture gets too thick to process. Remove from processor and mix in more bread crumbs until mixture becomes thick enough to form a ball. Place formed balls on a cookie sheet and bake for 10-15 minutes or until lightly browned. Serve hot or cold.

✍ COOL VEGETABLE MOLD ✍

¼ LB (113G)	BUTTER
½ CUP (125ML)	PURPLE ONION, MINCED
2 TBSP (30ML)	GARLIC, FINELY MINCED
1 TBSP (15ML)	FRESH PARSLEY, FINELY MINCED
1 TSP (5ML)	SALT
1 TSP (5ML)	PEPPER
1 QUART (1 LITER)	HEAVY CREAM
1 HEAD	BROCCOLI
1 TBSP (15ML)	PIMENTO
1 SMALL CAN	ASPARAGUS TIPS
1 TSP (5ML)	SUGAR
2 PACKAGES	UNFLAVORED GELATIN

(CONTINUES)

In a 2 quart saucepan melt butter and add onion, garlic and parsley. Saute' until onion begins to wilt. Add salt, pepper, heavy cream and stir in well. Bring to a low boil, reduce heat to low, cover and simmer for 5 minutes. Return to high heat, add broccoli florets, reduce heat to low and simmer for 15 minutes stirring frequently. Broccoli should be breaking up completely, if not, continue to simmer until this occurs. Add pimento and stir well. Next, add asparagus tips and sugar and stir very well. Remove from heat and leave covered until you are ready to add gelatin. Next, mix gelatin according to package instructions and add to vegetable mixture. Be sure to stir until completely blended. To a 1.5 quart (1.5 liter) mold, generously apply vegetable spray or liberally apply mayonnaise to the entire inside of the mold (don't worry if it clumps in the gaps) until completely covered. Add vegetable mixture to the mold. Place in refrigerator until set, about 6-8 hours. Serve.

❧ HOT BROCCOLI DIP ❧

2 TBSP (28G)	BUTTER	1 CUP (250ML)	CHICKEN STOCK
1 TBSP (15ML)	ALL-PURPOSE FLOUR	1½ CUPS (375ML)	CREAM OF MUSHROOM SOUP
1 LB (450G)	BROCCOLI, FROZEN CHOPPED	1 TBSP (15ML)	PARSLEY FLAKES
½ CUP (125ML)	MUSHROOM PIECES, CANNED	1 TSP (5ML)	TABASCO BRAND PEPPER SAUCE

(This is too easy) In a 1 quart (1 liter) saucepan, melt butter, add flour and whisk together well. Add thawed chopped broccoli and stir well. Drain canned mushroom pieces, add and stir well. Slowly add chicken stock, stirring until all is added. Bring mixture to a boil, reduce heat and simmer for 5 minutes on medium heat. Add cream of mushroom soup and stir well. Add the parsley flakes, salt, cayenne and TABASCO Sauce and stir well. Bring back to a low simmer, cover and simmer for 10 minutes. Serve hot with chips or french bread pieces.

✑ Hot Crab Dip ✑

¼ LB (113G)	BUTTER	1 TSP (5ML)	SALT	
2 TBSP (30ML)	ALL-PURPOSE FLOUR	½ TSP (2.5ML)	WHITE PEPPER	
2 CUPS (500ML)	HEAVY CREAM	½ LB (225G)	CREAM CHEESE	
1 TBSP (15ML)	WHOLE SWEET BASIL	1 LB (450G)	LUMP CRABMEAT,	
1 TSP (5ML)	GROUND THYME		CLEANED OF SHELL	

In a 2 quart (2 liter) skillet, melt butter and add flour. Whisk flour until completely blended with butter, add heavy cream a little at a time whisking constantly until blended with flour and butter. Keep heat on high and continue to whisk until mixture thickens. Add basil, thyme, salt and white pepper, whisk until blended. Bring mixture to a medium boil and slowly add cream cheese a little at a time whisking or stirring until blended. If mixture is too thick, add a little milk until mixture is perfect for dipping. Remove from heat, add all crabmeat. Stir gently until completely blended. Cover and allow to sit (off the stove) for 10 minutes. Serve with crackers or with pastry shells.

❧ NOTES ❧

_____

_____

_____

_____

_____

_____

_____

_____

_____

∾ Soups and Gumbo ∾

❧ SIZE OF PANS AND BAKING DISHES ❧

COMMON KITCHEN PANS TO USE AS CASSEROLES WHEN THE RECIPE CALLS FOR:

4 CUP BAKING DISH:
9-INCH PIE PLATE
8X1¼-INCH LAYER CAKE PAN
7⅞X3⅝X2¼-INCH LOAF PAN

6 CUP BAKING DISH:
8 OR 9X1½ INCH LAYER CAKE PAN
10-INCH PIE PLATE
8½X3⅝X2⅝-INCH LOAF PAN

8 CUP BAKING DISH:
8X8X2-INCH SQUARE PAN
11X7X1½-INCH BAKING PAN
9X5X3-INCH LOAF PAN

10 CUP BAKING DISH:
9X9X2-INCH SQUARE PAN
11¾X7½X1¾-INCH BAKING PAN
15X10X1-INCH JELLY-ROLL PAN

12 CUP BAKING DISH AND OVER:
13½X8½X2-INCH GLASS BAKING PAN, 12 CUPS
13X9X2-INCH METAL BAKING PAN, 15 CUPS
14X10½X2½-INCH ROASTING PAN, 19 CUPS

～ STOCKS ～

Stocks are a natural way to add both nutrition and flavor to any dish to which you would add water. When we cook we miss opportunities to make stocks out of what we would normally throw away.

The next time you trim meat, poultry or fish or any type of seafood or even the leftover vegies, don't throw them away. Just put them into a pot , cover with water and boil. Let the liquid cook and strain. It will usually take only 20-30 minutes of boiling to do the job.

After you strain the liquid, put back on high heat and cook down until the stock is concentrated into a thicker mixture. Then freeze what you don't use in ice trays and store in zip lock bags after the cubes are frozen. That way you can use it when you want in the amount you want.

If you are not cooking with stocks you are in for a real treat. Your soups, stews, gumbos and any other dish which requires water will taste like you got them from a restaurant.

∞ CHICKEN AND ANDOUILLE SAUSAGE GUMBO WITH TASSO ∞

2 LBS (900G)	ANDOUILLE SAUSAGE, OR PORK OR BEEF SAUSAGE	2 TBSP (30ML)	GARLIC, MINCED
2 WHOLE	CHICKEN FRYERS	1½ CUPS (375ML)	BELL PEPPER, CHOPPED MEDIUM
4 QTS (4 LTRS)	WATER, BECOMES CHICKEN STOCK	1 CUP (250ML)	TASSO, FINELY CHOPPED
1 CUP (250ML)	VEGETABLE OIL OR SHORTENING	2½-3QT (2.5-3 LTR)	CHICKEN STOCK, PROVIDED IN RECIPE
1½ CUPS (375ML)	ALL-PURPOSE FLOUR	2 CUPS (500ML)	OKRA, SLICED ¼" (6MM)
3 CUPS (750ML)	ONION, COARSLY CHOPPED	2 TBSP (30ML)	SALT
2 CUPS (500ML)	GREEN ONION, CHOPPED INCLUDING TOPS	1 TBSP (15ML)	BLACK PEPPER
		1 TBSP (15ML)	CAYENNE PEPPER
1 CUP (250ML)	CELERY, CHOPPED FINE	2 CUPS (500ML)	FRESH PARSLEY, FINELY CHOPPED

36

(CONTINUES)

Cut sausage into ⅜ inch slices. Boil chickens 40-50 minutes in water, cooking completely. Strain and reserve stock. Remove all meat from chickens, discard bones and skin.

Next, begin your roux in a 10 quart pot. Heat oil until it thins then add flour and stir on medium heat until the flour turns a dark brown (about the color of a dark tanned leather). Note: The roux may smoke some or even smell as though it is beginning to burn, but as long as you stir constantly and keep heat on medium you'll be okay. At this point, add onion, green onion, celery, garlic, bell pepper and Tasso, stirring into roux until onion begins to wilt; about 3 minutes. Add 2½ to 3 quarts of strained chicken stock and stir until mixed well.

Bring to bubble, about 10 minutes or so then add okra, salt, pepper, cayenne, parsley and sausage. Stir and cook 25 minutes. Stir in cooked chicken and simmer 5 more minutes. Remove from heat and serve over cooked rice.

As you have probably noticed, the potential for a very spicy dish exist here. Adjust the pepper either way to suit your taste. That is what Cajuns do – except they generally add pepper.

❧ Okra Seafood Gumbo ❧

6	Hardshell Gumbo Crabs, small	½ cup (375ml)	Whole Tomatoes, peeled & diced
2 qts (2 ltrs)	Water	2½-3 qt (2.5-3 ltr)	Crab or Seafood Stock
1 package	DryCrab Boil	3½ lbs (1.8kg)	Shrimp, peeled
¼ cup (63ml)	Bacon Fat	2 tsp (10ml)	Salt
3 lbs. (1.35kg)	Okra, chopped and destemmed	1 tsp (5ml)	Black Pepper
1 cup (250ml)	Vegetable Oil	1 tbsp (15ml)	Tabasco Brand Pepper Sauce
1½ cups (375ml)	All-Purpose Flour	1 tsp (5ml)	Ground Thyme
3 cups (750ml)	Onion, chopped medium	1	Bay Leaf
1 cup (250ml)	Green Onion, chopped	2 cups (500ml)	Cooked Ham, cubed, optional
2 tbsp (30ml)	Garlic, minced		
1 cup (250ml)	Bell Peppers, chopped		

38

(Continues)

First, boil crabs in 2 quarts of water and crab boil for 20 minutes. Do not add crabs until water is boiling. Live crabs are best. Reserve water.

Second, in a skillet, heat bacon fat, fry chopped okra on medium high heat, stirring constantly until it is brown and all the slime is gone, reserve.

Third, make your roux. In a large black iron or stainless steel pot, heat oil and add flour. Stir constantly until flour gets dark brown (about 20 minutes). Add onions, green onions and stir for 5 minutes. Add garlic, green pepper and tomatoes, stir for 2 minutes. Add stock (crab liquid from boiling) and enough water to make a thin consistency. Don't worry, it will be rich enough. Stir until all roux is mixed in. Be sure to add slowly and mix completely as you add liquid. Cover and simmer for 45-50 minutes stirring occasionally. Add shrimp, crabs, okra, salt, pepper, tabasco, thyme and bay leaf and cook 10 more minutes. Add ham and cook 10 more minutes. Serve over rice. Serves a bunch.

ARTICHOKE & OYSTER SOUP

¼ LB (113G)	BUTTER	10 DROPS	TABASCO BRAND PEPPER SAUCE
2 CUPS (500ML)	ONION, CHOPPED MEDIUM		
½ CUP (125ML)	CELERY, CHOPPED FINE	2 CUPS (500ML)	MARINATED ARTICHOKE HEARTS, PROCESSED FOR 10 SECONDS IN A FOOD PROCESSOR
2 TBSP (30ML)	GARLIC, MINCED		
¼ CUP (63ML)	ALL-PURPOSE FLOUR		
1 CUP (250ML)	HEAVY CREAM		
2 TBSP (30ML)	PARSLEY FLAKES	1 QT (1 LTR)	CHICKEN STOCK OR WATER
2 TBSP (30ML)	WHOLE SWEET BASIL	2 CUPS (500ML)	OYSTER LIQUEUR, STRAINED
1 TSP (5ML)	WHOLE THYME	24 MEDIUM	OYSTERS
2 TSP (10ML)	BLACK PEPPER	½ CUP (125ML)	GREEN ONION, CHOPPED
2 TSP (10ML)	SALT		

(CONTINUES)

In a 4 quart (4 liter) pot melt butter. Add onion, celery and garlic. Saute' for 5 minutes. Add flour and whisk until totally blended. Slowly add heavy cream a little at a time, whisking constantly until all is added. Continue to whisk until mixture begins to thicken. Add parsley, basil, thyme, pepper, salt, TABASCO, artichoke hearts, chicken stock and oyster liqueur. Stir well. Simmer on high until mixture begins to bubble. Reduce heat, cover and simmer for 35 minutes on low. Next, return heat to high and bring to a boil. Add oysters, stir well and maintain high heat until oysters begin to curl on the edges. Reduce heat to very low, cover and simmer for another 10 minutes. Add green onion, remove from heat, stir, cover and let stand for 10 minutes. Stir and serve. Serves 8.

❧ Vegetable Beef Soup ❧

4 QTS (4 LTRS)	BEEF STOCK, CHICKEN STOCK OR WATER	1 LB (450ML)	BAG MIXED VEGETABLES
		1 TSP (5ML)	GRANULATED GARLIC
2 LB (900G)	STEW BEEF, CUBED	½ TSP (2.5ML)	CAYENNE PEPPER
1 CUP (250ML)	ONION, CHOPPED COARSE	10 DROPS	TABASCO BRAND PEPPER SAUCE
2 CUPS (500ML)	STEWED CANNED TOMATOES, CHOPPED MEDIUM	¼ CUP (63ML)	FRESH PARSLEY, CHOPPED FINE
2 CUPS (500ML)	TOMATO SAUCE		
1 LB (450G)	RUSSET POTATOES, PEELED AND CUBED MEDIUM	2 TBSP (30ML)	FRESH BASIL, CHOPPED FINE
		2 TBSP	SALT
1 CUP (250ML)	CABBAGE, CHOPPED COARSE		GRATED ROMANO CHEESE FOR TOPPING
2 CUPS (500ML)	BABY STYLE CARROTS, WHOLE		
½ CUP (125ML)	CELERY, CHOPPED		

42

(CONTINUES)

In a 8 quart (8 liter) pot, heat 4 quarts of beefstock, chicken stock or water. Bring to a boil and add stew beef. Stir in well, bring back to a boil and continue to cook on medium high heat for approximately 40 minutes. Add onion, tomatoes, tomato sauce and bring to a boil for 5 minutes. Then add peeled potatoes, mix well and boil for 10 more minutes.

Next, add chopped cabbage and boil 10 more minutes. Add baby style carrots, celery and boil 10 more minutes.

Then add mixed vegetables, granulated garlic, cayenne, TABASCO, parsley, basil and salt and cook until vegetables are soft. Serve topped with grated romano cheese (optional). Serves 20.

ᴄᴓ MINESTRONE SOUP ᴓᴄ

1 LB (450G)	BEEF, GROUND	1 CUP (250ML)	RUSSET POTATOES, PEELED AND DICED
2 TSP (10ML)	CREOLE SEASONING, SEE SEASONING SECTION	1 CUP (250ML)	STEWED CANNED TOMATO, CUT INTO MEDIUM PIECES
2 TSP (10ML)	ITALIAN SEASONING	¼ CUP (63ML)	HOMINY, CANNED
1 CUP (250ML)	ONIONS, CHOPPED MEDIUM	¼ CUP (63ML)	PINTO BEANS, CANNED
1¾ QTS (1.75LTS)	CHICKEN STOCK OR WATER	1 CUP (80-90G)	ROTINI PASTA, PACKAGED & UNCOOKED
2 CUPS (500ML)	CABBAGE, CHOPPED MEDIUM	¼ CUP (63ML)	PARMESAN CHEESE, GRATED
1 CUP (250ML)	FRESH CARROTS, SLICED		

(CONTINUES)

In a 3 quart (3 liter) pot or larger, brown ground beef and drain. Add creole seasoning, italian seasoning, onion and saute' 5 minutes. Add stock or water and bring to boil.

Add cabbage, sliced frozen or fresh carrots, potatoes and stir well. Next, add tomatoes, stir well and bring to boil for 10 minutes. Add hominy, pinto beans and boil 30 minutes.

Add pasta and stir. Cook until noodles are 90% done. Remove from heat and add parmesan cheese and stir well. Serve. Serves 8.

CREAM OF BROCCOLI & ARTICHOKE SOUP

¼ LB (113G)	BUTTER	2 CUPS (500ML)	FROZEN BROCCOLI, CHOPPED
¼ CUP (63ML)	ALL-PURPOSE FLOUR		
1 TBSP (15ML)	SALT	1 CUP (250ML)	MARINATED ARTICHOKE HEARTS, QUARTERED
1 TBSP (15ML)	BLACK PEPPER		
2 CUPS (500ML)	WHOLE MILK	2 TBSP (30ML)	WHOLE SWEET BASIL
1 CUP (250ML)	HEAVY CREAM	1 TSP (5ML)	WHOLE THYME
1 CUP (250ML)	CHICKEN STOCK	1 TBSP (15ML)	GRANULATED GARLIC
½ CUP (125ML)	ONION, FINELY CHOPPED	1 TSP (5ML)	GRANULATED SUGAR

(CONTINUES)

In a 3 quart (3 liter) saucepan melt butter. Add flour, salt, pepper and whisk until totally blended. Slowly add milk until all is blended with flour mixture. Do the same with the heavy cream and then the chicken stock until both are totally blended. Add onion, broccoli and stir well. Reduce heat to low, cover and simmer for 15 minutes stirring frequently.

Add remaining ingredients, stirring after each is added. Return to high heat, stirring until mixture is bubbling. Reduce back to low, cover and simmer another 15 minutes, stirring every 5 minutes. If at any time mixture is sticking to the bottom of the pot then stir more frequently or reduce heat. Serves 6-8.

∽ SHRIMP AND CORN SOUP ∾

¼ LB (113G)	BUTTER	1 CUP (250ML)	ROTEL OR STEWED TOMATOES, DICED
2 CUPS (500ML)	ONION, CHOPPED MEDIUM	3 QTS (3 LTRS)	CHICKEN STOCK, SHRIMP STOCK OR WATER
1 CUP (250ML)	BELL PEPPER, CHOPPED MEDIUM	2 LG OR 3 MED	RUSSET POTATOES, PEELED AND DICED
½ CUP (125ML)	CELERY, CHOPPED FINE		
3 TBSP (45ML)	GARLIC, MINCED	2 CUPS (500ML)	WHOLE KERNEL CORN, FROZEN OR CANNED
1 CUP (250ML)	HAM OR TASSO, DICED		
3 TBSP (45ML)	FRESH PARSLEY, CHOPPED FINE	1 CUP (250ML)	CREAM STYLE CORN, CANNED
2 TBSP (30ML)	SALT	1 LB (450G)	SHRIMP, MEDIUM SIZED, PEELED & DEVEINED, USE THE PEEL TO MAKE THE STOCK
1 TBSP (15ML)	CREOLE SEASONING, SEE SEASONING SECTION		
1 TSP (5ML)	BLACK PEPPER	1 CUP (250ML)	GREEN ONION, CHOPPED

48

(CONTINUES)

In a 6 quart (6 Liter) pot, heat butter on high heat. When melted, add onion, bell pepper, celery, garlic, ham, parsley, salt, creole seasoning and black pepper and saute' for 10 minutes. Add Rotel tomatoes and bring to a bubble. Next, add stock or water, and bring to a rolling boil. Reduce heat to medium and add potatoes. Simmer on medium heat for 10 minutes. Add all corn and stir well. Bring back to a bubble, reduce heat to low and simmer for 15 minutes, stirring occasionally. Next, add shrimp and stir in well. Bring heat to high and bring to a low boil. Cover and reduce heat to low. Simmer for 5 minutes. Remove from heat and serve generously in large bowls topped with chopped green onion. Serves 12-15.

⨏ FRENCH ONION SOUP ⨎

¼ LB (113G)	BUTTER	1½ QTS (1.5 LTRS)	BEEF STOCK
3 VERY LARGE	ONIONS, SLICED ¼" (6MM) THICK	1 TSP. EACH	SALT AND PEPPER
2 TBSP (30ML)	ALL-PURPOSE FLOUR	¼ LOAF	FRENCH BREAD, CUBED
2 TBSP (30ML)	HALF AND HALF CREAM	½ CUP	MOZZARELLA, SHREDDED
		¼ CUP	PARMESAN, GRATED

In a 3 quart (3 liter) pot melt butter. Add onions and stir well. Cook until onions are soft and limp. Reduce heat. Saute' until onions begin to caramelize (moisture is gone and pan bottom and onions begin to brown). Add flour and stir until light brown in color.

Add half and half cream and whisk until completely blended and mixture begins to thicken. Add beef stock, salt, pepper and stir until blended. Bring to boil 10 minutes. Remove from heat, serve with cut up french bread and shredded mozzarella mixed with parmesan cheese. Serves 8.

✺ POULTRY ✺

⇜ POULTRY ROASTING GUIDE ⇝

TYPE OF POULTRY	READY-TO-COOK WEIGHT	OVEN TEMPERATURE	APPROXIMATE TOTAL ROASTING TIME
TURKEY	6 TO 8 LBS	325°	2½ TO 3 HOURS
	8 TO 12 LBS	325°	3 TO 3½ HOURS
	12 TO 16 LBS	325°	3½ TO 4 HOURS
	16 TO 20 LBS	325°	4 TO 4½ HOURS
	20 TO 24 LBS	300°	5 TO 6 HOURS
CHICKEN, UNSTUFFED	2 TO 2½ LBS	400°	1 TO 1½ HOURS
	2½ TO 4 LBS	400°	1½ TO 2½ HOURS
	4 TO 8 LBS	325°	3 TO 5 HOURS
DUCK, UNSTUFFED	3 TO 5 LBS	325°	2½ TO 3 HOURS

NOTE: SMALL CHICKENS ARE ROASTED TO 400° SO THAT THEY BROWN WELL IN THE SHORT COOKING TIME. THEY MAY ALSO BE DONE AT 325 BUT WILL TAKE LONGER AND WILL NOT BE AS BROWN. INCREASE COOKING TIME 15 TO 20 MINUTES FOR STUFFED CHICKEN AND DUCK.

᥍ Chicken Sausage Jambalaya ᥍

10½ CUPS (2 LTRS+625ML)	CHICKEN STOCK
¼ CUP (63ML)	DARK BROWN ROUX
2 TBSP (30ML)	SALT
¼ LB (113G)	BUTTER
6 CUPS (1.5 LITERS)	ONION, CHOPPED MEDIUM
3 CUPS (750ML)	BELL PEPPER, CHOPPED MEDIUM
1½ CUPS (375ML)	CELERY, CHOPPED FINE
3 TBSP (45ML)	GARLIC, MINCED
¼ CUP (63ML)	DRIED PARSLEY FLAKES
3 TBSP (45ML)	WHOLE SWEET BASIL
¼ CUP (63ML)	CREOLE SEASONING, SEE SEASONING SECTION
1 CUP (250ML)	GROUND TASSO OR HAM

(CONTINUES)

3 CUPS (750ML)	CRUSHED TOMATO, CANNED, OR 6 CUPS (1.5LTS.) FRESH CHOPPED TOMATO
½ CUP (125ML)	TOMATO PASTE, ¾ CUP IF USING FRESH TOMATO
5 CUPS (1KG)	SMOKED PORK SAUSAGE, SLICE ¼" (.75MM)
4-6 CUPS (2 LB OR 900G)	BONELESS CHICKEN, CUT TO DESIRED SIZE
5 CUPS (1.25LT)	LONG GRAIN OR CONVERTED RICE
1 CUP	GREEN ONION, CHOPPED

In a 4 quart (4 liter) saucepan, heat chicken stock on high heat until a rolling boil. Add roux and stir until totally dissolved. Boil on high (as high as you can without boiling over) for 15-20 minutes. Add salt and stir well.

Meanwhile, in a 12 quart (12 liter) pot, heat butter on high heat until totally melted and bubbly. Add onion, bell pepper, celery, garlic, parsley, basil, Creole seasoning and stir well. Saute' on high until onions begin to wilt. If using Tasso, add now and stir well. Saute'

(CONTINUES)

another 5 minutes. Add crushed tomato and stir well. Bring back to bubble and add tomato paste, stir until totally blended. Add boiled out chicken stock to 6 quart (6 liter) pot and stir well. Bring to rolling boil. Taste the mixture to test for seasoning. Mixture should be slightly too salty. If not, add salt and stir well. Add pork sausage and stir well. Cook on high heat for 10 minutes stirring occasionally.

Next, add cooked chicken and stir in well. Bring back to boil and add uncooked rice to pot and stir well. Bring to rolling boil, stir well, cover and simmer on low heat for 10 minutes. Stir and cover for 5 minutes. Continue process until rice is 95% cooked. Cover and remove from heat, let stand for at least 10 minutes. Add chopped green onion and stir well. Serve.

❧ Chicken Spaghetti Creole ❧

OR YOU COULD SAY ITALIAN. THE FLAIR OF THIS DISH IS BORN OF THE ITALIAN INFLUENCE ON NEW ORLEANS STYLE COOKING. WE JUST LIKE TO SPICE IT MORE THAN THE USUAL ITALIAN STYLE, AND IT MAKES YOUR MOUTH HAPPY.

2	WHOLE CHICKEN FRYERS,	1 CUP (250ML)	BELL PEPPER, CHOPPED
3 TBSP (45ML)	OLIVE OIL	1 CUPS (250ML)	TOMATO PASTE
3 TBSP (45ML)	VEGETABLE OIL	2 CUPS (500ML)	CHICKEN STOCK
2 CUPS (500ML)	ONION, CHOPPED	2 CUPS (500ML)	TOMATO SAUCE
1 TBSP (15ML)	GARLIC, MINCED	1 TBSP (15ML)	SUGAR
¼ CUP (63ML)	PARSLEY FLAKES	1 LB (450G)	SPAGHETTI
½ CUP (125ML)	GREEN ONION WITH TOPS,	2 TBSP (30ML)	SALT
½ CUP (125ML)	GREEN ONION, CHOPPED		

(CONTINUES)

Cut chickens into 8 pieces each. In a 12 quart (12 liter) pot add chicken pieces and cover with water. Heat to boil and cook for 30 minutes. Reserve stock. Save chicken for later.

In the same pot, heat olive oil and vegetable oil on medium/high heat. Add onion, garlic, parsley, green onion and bell pepper. Simmer for 5 minutes, reduce heat to medium/low. Add tomato paste and stir. Slowly add chicken stock until mixed well. Raise heat to medium/high. Add chicken parts, tomato sauce and stir. Add sugar, stir, cover and reduce heat to simmer. Cook for 35 minutes. Serve over spaghetti.

To cook spaghetti boil water in an 8 quart (8 liter) pot. Add salt and spaghetti to boiling water. Return to a boil, stir spaghetti, cover and simmer for 18 minutes. Drain and serve. Serves 8.

∽ Duck Etouffee ∾

1	Domestic Duck
¼ lb (113g)	Butter
¼ cup (63ml)	All-Purpose Flour
2 cups (500ml)	Onion, chopped
1 cup (250ml)	Bell Pepper, chopped
½ cup (125ml)	Celery, chopped
¼ cup (63ml)	Garlic, minced
2 tbsp (30ml)	Parsley Flakes
1 tbsp (15ml)	Creole Seasoning
or 1 tsp (5ml)	Each Salt, Cayenne and Black Pepper
1 tbsp (15ml)	Whole Sweet Basil
3 cups (750ml)	Duck Stock, provided in the recipe

(Continues)

Clean and cut duck into pieces. Save all internal parts as well as the neck and all pieces trimmed from the pieces cut for use in the dish. In a 2 quart (2 liter) pot place all throw away pieces into pot and cover with 1 quart (1 liter) water. Heat on high until boiling. Boil for 45 minutes. Strain, discard bones and other debris and let cool. Skim off grease and reserve for etouffee'.

In a 4 quart (4 liter) pot heat olive oil and place all saved pieces of duck in hot oil. Brown on both sides and remove from pan. Reserve. Next, melt butter on high. Add flour to butter and whisk until brown (the color of paper bags). Next, add onion, bell pepper, celery, garlic, parsley flakes, creole seasoning and basil and stir well. Saute' until onions begin to wilt, stirring frequently.

Next, add 3 cups (750ml) reserved duck stock a little at a time stirring and blending as you add. Continue to stir until completely blended. Bring to a bubble, cover and reduce heat and simmer for 10 minutes. Add browned duck pieces and stir well. Cover and simmer for 35 minutes, stirring occasionally. Serve over rice or pasta.

❧ TURKEY PIE ❧

2 TBSP (30ML)	OLIVE OIL	2 TBSP (30ML)	ALL-PURPOSE FLOUR
½ CUP (125ML)	ONIONS, CHOPPED	2 CUPS (500ML)	COOKED TURKEY MEAT, DICED
¼ CUP (63ML)	BELL PEPPER, CHOPPED		
2 TBSP (30ML)	CELERY, CHOPPED	2 CUPS (500ML)	MILK OR HALF AND HALF CREAM
1 TBSP (15ML)	GARLIC, MINCED		
1 TBSP (15ML)	PARSLEY FLAKES	½ CUP (125ML)	PEAS, FROZEN
1 TSP (5ML)	EACH SALT AND BLACK PEPPER	¼ CUP (63ML)	CARROTS, COOKED

In a 2 quart (2 liter) saucepan heat oil to hot. Add onion, bell pepper, celery, garlic, parsley flakes, salt and pepper and saute' until onion begins to wilt. Next, add flour and stir in well. Stir in turkey meat and bring mixture to hot. Slowly add milk and stir until totally blended. Bring to a boil, reduce heat, add peas, carrots and stir well. Cover and simmer (on low) for 20 minutes.

(CONTINUES)

PIE CRUST:

2¼ CUPS (563ML)	ALL-PURPOSE FLOUR	¾ CUP (175ML)	BUTTER FLAVORED SHORTENING
1 TSP (5ML)	SALT	ABOUT ½ CUP	WATER, ICE COLD

In a bowl mix flour, salt and shortening with a whisk or your hands until blended. Dough should form small pea-sized balls. Next, sprinkle water over flour and blend with a fork or large spoon until completely blended. Turn dough over a floured surface and knead until dough is silky. Cut out ⅓ of dough and reserve. Roll out ⅔ of dough on floured surface until able to fill a 12" x 12" (27.5cm x 27.5cm) pan that is 2" (5cm) deep. Place rolled dough into pan centered and able to fit firmly against the sides and hang over the edges.

Next, put turkey filling into pie. Roll out the other ⅓ of dough and place on top of filling to completely cover the pan and hang over the sides. Using roller, press dough to the edges of the pan, cutting off the excess and sealing the pie. Cut slits in the top to allow steam to escape. Bake in a 350°F (175°C) pre-heated oven for 35 to 40 minutes or until crust is golden brown.

ᥬ Chicken Dijon ᥬ

¼ CUP (113G)	BUTTER
4 BONED	CHICKEN BREASTS
3 TBSP (45ML)	ALL-PURPOSE FLOUR
3 CUPS (750ML)	HEAVY CREAM
½ CUP (125ML)	ONION, FINELY CHOPPED
¼ CUP (63ML)	CELERY, MINCED VERY FINE
3 TBSP (45ML)	GARLIC, MINCED
1 TBSP (15ML)	WHOLE SWEET BASIL
1 TSP (5ML)	CRUSHED ROSEMARY
½ CUP (125ML)	CHICKEN STOCK, CONCENTRATED
¼ CUP (63ML)	DIJON MUSTARD

(CONTINUES)

In a 10" (25cm) skillet, heat butter to hot, add chicken breasts and simmer on medium high until 90% cooked. Remove chicken and reserve. Add flour and whisk into butter. Immediately add heavy cream and whisk until blended. As soon as mixture begins to thicken, add onion, celery, garlic, whole sweet basil, rosemary, concentrated chicken stock and dijon mustard and stir until completely blended. Bring back to a bubble, cover and reduce heat to low. Simmer for 20 minutes stirring frequently. Add reserved chicken, maintain low heat, cover and simmer for another 20 minutes stirring occasionally. Serve over your favorite pasta or with potato.

❧ MARINATED GRILLED CHICKEN BREAST ❧

4	CHICKEN BREASTS, SKINNED AND BONED
¼ CUP (63ML)	WHITE WINE
1 TBSP (15ML)	WORCESTERSHIRE SAUCE
1 TBSP (15ML)	GARLIC, PRESSED OR JUICE
1 TSP (5ML)	TABASCO BRAND PEPPER SAUCE
¼ CUP (56G)	BUTTER
	SALT AND PEPPER TO TASTE

Clean chicken breasts and pat dry. With the tip of a knife punch the top of each breast several times from end to end. Place in marinade container. In a food processor, (if you don't have a food processor a wire whisk will serve the purpose) place white wine, worcestershire sauce, garlic, TABASCO and process for 30 seconds. Pour over chicken breasts. With your

(CONTINUES)

hands mix well with the chicken, making sure that chicken is completely covered. Place in refrigerator, over night if possible. Allow chicken to marinate for at least 4 hours.

To grill the chicken, heat a 10" (25cm) skillet to hot and add all butter in 1 tbsp (14g) pieces. Move pan to distribute butter and complete the melting. You may have to remove the pan from the fire to do so if the pan is sizzling too much. Return to heat. Remove chicken breasts from marinade and allow excess to drip off. Place all chicken in skillet, sprinkle with salt and pepper to taste and allow to cook on high heat until you can see white begin to show through the middle of the chicken breast. Flip breasts over with a spatula, and cook until brown on the other side. This process should take only 4 to 6 minutes. Serve.

✺ COQ AU VIN • CHICKEN IN WINE SAUCE ✺

6	CHICKEN BREASTS, BONELESS AND SKINLESS
½ CUP (113G)	BUTTER
½ CUP (125ML)	GREEN ONION, FINELY CHOPPED
1 TSP (5ML)	WHOLE THYME
1 TSP (5ML)	WHOLE BASIL
1	BAY LEAF
1 TSP (5ML)	BLACK PEPPER
2 CUPS (500ML)	QUALITY WHITE WINE
2 TBSP (57G)	BUTTER
¼ CUP (63ML)	ONION, FINELY CHOPPED
2 TBSP (30ML)	ALL-PURPOSE FLOUR
1 CUP (250ML)	FRESH MUSHROOMS, QUARTERED

(CONTINUES)

Preheat oven to 350°F (175°C). In a large skillet melt ½ cup (113g) butter, add chicken breasts. Cook on high heat to brown both sides of the chicken. After turning chicken once add green onion, thyme, basil, bay leaf and pepper. Remove chicken and saute' green onion for one minute. Place chicken into a large oven pan. Add wine to butter mixture and saute until combined then pour over the chicken. Cover with foil, place in oven and bake for 50 minutes.

Meanwhile, in the same skillet melt remaining butter and add onion and saute' for 5 minutes. Add flour and whisk until flour is almost a paper bag color. Remove from heat and continue to whisk until pan cools slightly. Mixture should have darkened some more. Reserve.

When chicken is done, remove from oven. Remove chicken and reserve. Place pan on burner on high heat. As soon as mixture begins to bubble slowly add the flour mixture, whisking as you add until all is added. Continue to whisk until mixture thickens. Return chicken to pan, reduce heat and saute' for 2 minutes. Remove from heat, cover and let stand for 3 minutes. Serve.

∾ New Orleans Baked Chicken ∾

1	Chicken Fryer,		Salt and Pepper to taste
	reserve inner packet	¼ cup (56g)	Butter
2 medium	Onions, peeled	2 cups (500ml)	Water

Pre-heat oven to 350°F (175°C). Place peeled onions (cut up or whole) into the cavity of a completely washed chicken. Place chicken into a 9" x 9" (22.5cm x 22.5cm) baking pan that is at least 2" (5cm) deep. Place butter, water and whole innards into the water. Sprinkle salt and pepper to taste over chicken. Cover with foil and bake for 45 minutes. Spray the inside of the foil with vegetable spray to avoid sticking.

After 45 minutes remove foil, check that there is at least ½" (1.25cm) water in pan, raise heat to 400°F (205°C) and bake another 15 minutes or until chicken is brown. Serve.

❧ Beef and Pork ❧

❧ TOTAL VOLUME OF VARIOUS SPECIAL BAKING PANS ❧

TUBE PANS:	7½x3-inch "BUNDT" TUBE PAN	6 CUPS
	9x3½-inch FANCY TUBE OR "BUNDT" PAN	9 CUPS
	9x3½-inch ANGEL CAKE PAN	12 CUPS
	10x3¾-inch "BUNDT" OR "CROWNBURST" PAN	12 CUPS
	9x3½-inch FANCY TUBE MOLD	12 CUPS
	10x4-inch FANCY TUBE MOLD (KUGELHUPF)	16 CUPS
	10x4-inch ANGEL CAKE PAN	18 CUPS
MELON MOLD:	7x5½x4-inch MOLD	6 CUPS
SPRING-FORM PANS:	8x3-inch PAN	12 CUPS
	9x3-inch PAN	16 CUPS
RING MOLDS:	8½x2¼-inch MOLD	4½ CUPS
	9¼x2¾-inch MOLD	8 CUPS
CHARLOTTE MOLD:	6x4¼-inch MOLD	7½ CUPS
BRIOCHE PAN:	9½x3¼-inch PAN	8 CUPS

✂ Ribs, Ribs, Ribs, oh man! Ribs ✄

1 SLAB	PORK RIBS, CUT, CRACKED AND TRIMMED	1 CUP (250ML)	TOMATO SAUCE
½ CUP (125ML)	PORK FAT	½ CUP (125ML)	WORCESTERSHIRE SAUCE
2 CUPS (500ML)	ONION, CHOPPED MEDIUM	¼ CUP (63ML)	VINEGAR
2 CUPS (500ML)	CRUSHED TOMATO	¼ CUP (63ML)	SUGAR
		2 TBSP (30ML)	LEMON

Place cut and trimmed ribs into an 8 quart pot and cover with water. Place on high heat and bring to boil. Boil for 15 minutes. Remove from liquid and reserve.

In a 2 quart saucepan heat pork fat. Add onion and saute' until onions begin to brown. Add crushed tomato and stir in well. Add tomato sauce and stir well. Add remaining ingredients and whisk until completely blended. Bring to a boil, stirring frequently. Remove from heat. In a 2" (5cm) baking pan arrange ribs until all are added. Pour reserved sauce over ribs and bake at 275°F (135°C) for 1 hour. Serve.

❧ ROAST PORK ❧

1 6-8 LB.(2.5-3.5 KG)	PORK BUTT, TRIMMED OF FAT
½ CUP (125ML)	OLIVE OIL
½ CUP (125ML)	ALL-PURPOSE FLOUR
4 CUPS (1LT)	ONIONS, CHOPPED COURSE
2 TBSP (30ML)	GARLIC, MINCED
½ CUP (125ML)	FRESH PARSLEY, FINELY CHOPPED
1 TSP (5ML)	SALT
1 TBSP (15ML)	BLACK PEPPER
3 CUPS (750ML)	WATER

Clean roast of most exterior fat. Cut bone out (Its okay if the pork is cut up a little after cutting bone out). In a large pot heat oil on high heat. Place roast and any pieces in the pot with hot oil. Turn pork several times until browned on all sides. Reduce heat to medium

(CONTINUES)

low. Cover and simmer for 1½ hours, turning roast every 20 minutes. Remove roast to cutting board. Raise heat to high and add flour to oil and drippings. Stir until flour browns to a medium brown color. Add onion, garlic, parsley, salt and pepper and stir constantly for 10 minutes. Reduce heat, cover and simmer for 5 minutes. Meanwhile cut pork roast into 2 or 3 inch (5 to 7.5 cm) cubes. Add water a little at a time stirring constantly, until all water is added. Add pork to pot, mix well and cover. Simmer 20 minutes stirring occasionally. Simmer 10 more minutes. Serve over rice or with potatoes. Serves 6-8.

CREOLE STYLE MEAT LOAF

1 LB. (450G)	BEEF, GROUND	2 TBSP (30ML)	PREPARED YELLOW, MUSTARD
1 LB. (450G)	PORK, GROUND		
1½ CUPS (375ML)	ONION, CHOPPED	3 TBSP (45ML)	KETCHUP
½ CUP (125ML)	GREEN ONION, CHOPPED, INCLUDE TOPS	¼ CUP (63ML)	FRESH TOMATO, SEEDED AND FINELY CHOPPED
2 TBSP (30ML)	GARLIC, MINCED	2 TBSP (30ML)	WORCESTERSHIRE SAUCE
¼ CUP (63ML)	FRESH PARSLEY, CHOPPED	1 TBSP (15ML)	SALT
2	EGGS, SLIGHTLY SCRAMBLED	1 TSP (5ML)	SUGAR
1½ CUPS (375ML)	ITALIAN BREAD CRUMBS	1 TBSP (15ML)	BLACK PEPPER

THE GRAVY:

3 TBSP (45ML)	FAT DRIPPINGS, FROM MEATLOAF	2 CUPS	WATER OR BEEF STOCK PREFERRED
3 TBSP (45ML)	ALL-PURPOSE FLOUR		

(CONTINUES)

Pre-heat oven to 350°F (175°C). In a large bowl combine ground beef and ground pork. Add onion, green onion, garlic and parsley and mix well (your hands work best to mix). Add eggs and mix further. Add bread crumbs, mustard, ketchup, tomato, worcestershire sauce, salt, sugar and pepper. Complete the mixing (Note: you can add or subtract the bread crumbs to get the consistency you like). Next, in a baking pan, shape into a loaf and be creative. Cover and put into 350°F (175°C) oven for 45 minutes. Next, remove cover and bake at same temperature for another 15 minutes. Remove loaf from pan. Drain off excess oil but be sure to leave about 3-4 tbsp (45 to 60ml) on the side to make the gravy.

THE GRAVY:

In a skillet heat reserved drippings on medium high heat. Mix flour in 2 cups of water or beef stock. When pan is sizzling and bubbling add flour and begin stirring with a flat wooden or plastic spatula. Scrap the bottom completely as you are stirring and do so until gravy thickens. Serve over meat loaf, rice or potatoes. If gravy is too thick for your taste, just add water or stock while you are stirring. This dish serves 8 people.

❧ STUFFED POT OR OVEN ROAST ❧

1 6-7 LB. (3KG)	RUMP ROAST, OR YOUR FAVORITE CUT OF BEEF	2 CUPS (500ML)	ONION, CHOPPED
		1 TBSP (15ML)	GARLIC, MINCED
2 TBSP (30ML)	OLIVE OIL	1 TSP (5ML)	SALT
3 TBSP (45ML)	PARSLEY FLAKES	1 TSP (5ML)	BLACK PEPPER
10 CLOVES	GARLIC, SLICED ⅟₁₆" (5MM)	3 TBSP (45ML)	ALL-PURPOSE FLOUR
1 TBSP (15ML)	OLIVE OIL, FOR THE POT VERSION ONLY	1 CUP (250ML)	WATER
		1 CUP (250ML)	CREAM OF MUSHROOM SOUP
2 CUPS (500ML)	BEEF STOCK OR WATER		

Mix olive oil, parsley flakes and sliced garlic in a small bowl. Mix well and allow to stand for 15 minutes before using to stuff the roast. This is the mixture that will be put into the slits made in the roast, as described below.

72

(CONTINUES)

Clean roast and trim off the thick slab of fat on the bottom with a sharp filet knife. With a pairing knife make thin, narrow deep cuts into the roast. As you cut slits in the roast, push your finger into cuts to open inside pockets. Stuff garlic mixture into cuts. Do so several times all around the roast until mixture is gone. With remaining oil and parsley in the mixture, coat the roast and salt the meat lightly.

FOR THE POT ROAST VERSION:

If you are cooking in a pot, choose one with a good cover. Heat oil on high heat. Brown all sides of the roast. Add 2 cups (500ml) water, onion, minced garlic, salt and pepper. Cover and simmer on low heat for 25 minutes for each pound of roast. When roast is finished, take the roast out of the pot and place on a cutting board. Mix flour in 1 cup (250ml) water and bring heat to high. When bubbly, slowly stir in flour and water mixture (Note: make sure flour is completely mixed). Stir until mixture thickens. Add cream of mushroom soup and stir in well. Bring to a bubble and reduce heat to simmer. Cover and simmer 5 minutes. You may want to add sliced roast beef to the gravy before serving.

(CONTINUES)

Preheat oven to 275°F (135°C). Prepare roast with stuffing as described above. Place roast in baking pan. Put in 2 cups water, onion, minced garlic, salt and pepper. Stir into water so that seasoning is evenly distributed in the pan. Cover and put into pre-heated oven. Every 30 minutes baste the roast until it has cooked 30 minutes for each pound (½ kg) of beef (Note: In either case, if you have a cooking thermometer, the center should read 190-200°F (88-96°C) for well done. When cooked remove roast to cutting board. Place pan on stove burner and heat on high. When bubbly, mix flour in 1 cup (250ml) beef stock or water until mixed well. Stir into gravy slowly and consistently until all has been added. Simmer 5 minutes. Add cream of mushroom soup and stir until mixture is consistent in texture. Reduce heat and simmer 5 minutes. Again you may want to add sliced roast to the gravy.

Additional Note: In either case the gravy is great over rice or creamed or baked potato. Serves 8-10.

✄ PORK POT ROAST ✄

1 4-5 LB. (3-5KG)	PORK BUTT	1 CUP (250ML)	CARROT, CUT 1" LENGTHS
1 TBSP (15ML)	OLIVE OIL	1 LARGE	BELL PEPPER, CUBED
1 TSP (15ML)	SALT		1" SQUARE
1 TSP (15ML)	PEPPER	1 QUART (1LTR)	WATER
1 CUP (250ML)	ONION, QUARTERED		

Trim fat from pork butt. With your hands, coat the roast with the olive oil then salt and pepper.

In a 10 quart (10 liter) pot, place roast in pot on high heat. Brown all sides. Add onion, carrot, bell pepper and water and stir well. Bring water to a boil. Cover and reduce heat to low. Simmer for 2-2½ hours, or until meat is tender enough to pull a piece off and taste. If you have a meat thermometer the center should be 180-190°F (80-90°C). Remove from pot and allow to cool. Meanwhile add enough water to bring back to 1 quart, heat to boiling. Slice pork to desired thickness and add to the pot. Heat and serve.

✍ BLACKENED RIB EYE ✍

BECAUSE THE COOKING PROCESS IS VERY FAST IN THIS RECIPE, THICKNESS IS THE ONLY WAY TO ACHIEVE THE DESIRED STAGE OF COOKING. USE THE SUGGESTED CHART BELOW TO CHOOSE THE CORRECT THICKNESS OF YOUR STEAK. ADDITIONAL NOTE: BE SURE TO HAVE GREAT VENTILATION BEFORE COOKING. I SUGGEST YOU DO THIS OUTSIDE IF POSSIBLE SINCE BUTTER WILL SMOKE AND POP DURING THE COOKING PROCESS.

UP TO ¼" (7MM)	WELL DONE
UP TO ⅜" (10MM)	MEDIUM WELL DONE
UP TO ½" (13MM)	MEDIUM DONE
UP TO ⅝" (16MM)	MEDIUM RARE DONE
UP TO ¾" (19MM)	RARE DONE
UP TO 1" (2.54CM)	VERY RARE DONE

(CONTINUES)

2	RIB EYE STEAKS, CUT TO DESIRED THICKNESS	1½ TSP (7.5ML)	PAPRIKA
		1½ TSP (7.5ML)	SALT
1 TBSP (15ML)	CAYENNE PEPPER	1½ TSP (7.5ML)	BLACK PEPPER
1 TBSP (15ML)	WHOLE OREGANO	¼ CUP (57G)	BUTTER
1½ TSP (7.5ML)	CRUSHED ROSEMARY		

Clean steaks and pat dry. Mix cayenne pepper, oregano, rosemary, paprika, salt and black pepper in a bowl until completely blended. Next, sprinkle mixture over both sides of the steak until completely coated. Heat skillet to hot and add 2 tbsp (28g) of butter to the pan. Butter will smoke and pop and turn slightly brown. Lift the skillet off of the fire and move the butter around until almost melted. Next, place back on fire and as soon as the butter begins to smoke again place both steaks in the butter for 60 seconds each side. Remove steaks from pan and add remaining butter scraping the bottom as you stir in the butter. As soon as the butter is melted pour over each steak and serve.

✆ Pane'd Pork Chops ✆

6	Thin Center Cut Pork Chops, trimmed of all fat
1	Egg, scrambled
¼ cup (63ml)	Whole Milk
1 tsp (5ml)	Salt
1 tsp (5ml)	Black Pepper
1 tbsp (15ml)	Parsley Flakes
½ tsp (2.5ml)	Whole Sage
1-1½ cups (375ml)	Italian Seasoned Bread Crumbs
½" (13mm)	Peanut or Canola Oil in a skillet for frying

(Continues)

Wash pork chops well and pat dry. In a bowl whisk egg, whole milk, salt, black pepper, parsley flakes and sage until completely blended. Note: this would be a good time to put the oil on the fire. I suggest a 10" (25cm) skillet with ½" (13mm) of oil for frying, on high heat. Meanwhile, sprinkle about ½ of bread crumbs in a large platter. Dip pork chops, one at a time, into the egg mixture and then set down onto the bread crumbs until all are on the platter. Sprinkle remaining bread crumbs over pork chops and pat down. Turn pork chops over and over until completely coated. Next, test oil heat by sprinkling a small amount of bread crumbs into oil. If it bubbles immediately oil is hot enough for frying. Carefully place pork chops in the hot oil until all are in the pan. Turn chops over several times until nicely brown on both sides. Remove to paper towels to drain and serve.

✂ Stuffed Pork Chops ✂

4-2" (5.08CM)	PORK CHOPS, CENTER CUT
1 TSP (5ML)	EACH SALT AND BLACK PEPPER
½ LB (225G)	PORK, GROUND
¼ CUP (63ML)	ONION, FINELY CHOPPED
1 TBSP (15ML)	GARLIC, FINELY MINCED
2 TBSP (30ML)	GREEN ONION, FINELY CHOPPED
1 TBSP (15ML)	FRESH PARSLEY, FINELY CHOPPED
½ TSP (2.5ML)	SALT
½ TSP (2.5ML)	BLACK PEPPER
1 TSP (5ML)	PAPRIKA
½ TSP (2.5ML)	GROUND SAGE
½ TSP (2.5ML)	GROUND FENNEL SEED

Wash pork chops, pat dry and sprinkle with 1 tsp (5ml) salt and black pepper. Next, with a sharp filet or paring knife, trim off excess fat. Cut a 1" (2.54cm) slit into the middle of the front of the pork chop from side to side. Use the slit to cut a pocket into the pork chop from the bone to about ½" (13mm) from the end of the meat creating a complete pocket in each pork chop (Note: your butcher will do this for you if you request it). Next, in a large bowl mix ground pork with all remaining ingredients until all is mixed and blended well.

Preheat oven to 350°F (175°C). Stuff the ground pork mixture into the pockets of the pork chops. Be generous and stuff it in until pork chop expands in the center. Do this until all are stuffed. If there is any stuffing left just make them into balls and cook with the pork chops. Next, spray an oven pan with a vegetable coating and place pork chops into pan with 1 cup (250ml) water and cover. Place in oven for 35 minutes, remove cover and bake another 15 minutes. Serve.

∽ SMOTHERED SALISBURY STEAK ∾

1 LB (450G)	BEEF GROUND ROUND
½ CUP (125ML)	ONION, FINELY CHOPPED
¼ CUP (63ML)	BELL PEPPER, FINELY CHOPPED
1 TBSP (15ML)	GARLIC, FINELY MINCED
1 TBSP (15ML)	PARSLEY FLAKES
1 TBSP (15ML)	WORCESTERSHIRE SAUCE
1 TBSP (15ML)	PREPARED YELLOW MUSTARD
1	EGG, SLIGHTLY SCRAMBLED
1 TSP (5ML)	EACH SALT AND BLACK PEPPER
1½ CUPS (375ML)	ITALIAN SEASONED BREAD CRUMBS
2 TBSP (30ML)	ALL-PURPOSE FLOUR
2 CUPS (500ML)	BEEF STOCK OR WATER
¼ LB (113G)	BUTTER
3	LARGE ONIONS, CUT INTO RINGS

(CONTINUES)

In a large bowl mix ground beef with chopped onion, bell pepper, garlic, parsley flakes, worcestershire sauce, prepared yellow mustard, egg and italian seasoned bread crumbs. Mix until mixture will hold together to form ovals.

Place shaped steaks into a skillet on medium high heat and brown on all sides. While steaks are browning, in a separate 2 quart saucepan melt butter and saute' onion rings until just beginning to brown. Set aside.

When steaks are brown remove to a platter. Pour out ½ of the oil, then place flour in remaining oil and stir well. Continue to stir until flour browns the color of peanut butter. Add beef stock or water a little at a time stirring constantly until all is added. Return steaks to skillet and bring to a bubble. Add onions and butter to skillet, cover and simmer on low for 25 minutes. Serve.

❧ Round Steak Roulades ❧

1	WHOLE ROUND STEAK, CUT TO ⅜" (9MM) THICK
¼ LB (62.5ML)	BEEF GROUND ROUND
¼ LB (62.5ML)	BREAKFAST SAUSAGE, GROUND PORK
½ CUP (125ML)	ONION, FINELY CHOPPED
2 TBSP (30ML)	GARLIC, MINCED
1 TSP (5ML)	EACH SALT AND BLACK PEPPER
1 TSP (5ML)	GROUND ROSEMARY
1 TBSP (15ML)	WHOLE BASIL
	PAN SPRAY
1 CUP (250ML)	WATER

(CONTINUES)

Cut round steak into sections following the natural patterns of the meat being sure to remove all excess fat and membrane as well as the small center bone (if there). Some of the pieces of meat will be too small to use, but make sure you have pieces at least 4" (about 10cm) long and 3" (about 7.5cm) wide. When pieces of meat are cut to that size, place in a zip lock bag or folded into clear wrap and pound to flat and thin with a meat mallet, reserve meat.

Next, mix ground beef, ground pork breakfast sausage, onion, garlic, salt, black pepper, rosemary and whole basil in a bowl until completely blended. Preheat oven to 350°F (175°C). Lay pieces of pounded round on a board and place an ample amount of the ground meat mixture on them and roll the meat over. Place rolls of meat in a pan sprayed with pan spray. Put water in pan, cover and bake in pre-heated oven for 30 minutes, uncover and continue to bake another 10 minutes. Serve.

_____

_____

_____

_____

_____

_____

_____

_____

∽ NOTES ∾

∽ IDANO ∽

❧ Substitutions for a Missing Ingredient ❧

1 Square Chocolate, 1 ounce..3 or 4 tbsp cocoa plus ½ tbsp fat
1 tbsp Cornstarch, for thickening...2 tbsp flour
1 cup All Purpose Flour, sifted....................................1 cup plus 2 tbsp sifted cake flour
1 cup Cake Flour, sifted ....1 cup minus 2 tbsp sifted all purpose flour
1 tsp Baking Powder.......................................¼ tsp baking soda plus ½ tsp cream of tartar
1 cup Sour Milk... 1 cup buttermilk, let stand for 5 minutes
.........or 1 cup sweet milk into which 1 tbsp vinegar or lemon juice has been stirred
1 cup Sweet Milk...................1 cup sour milk or buttermilk plus ½ tsp baking soda
¾ cup Cracker Crumbs...1 cup bread crumbs
1 cup Cream, sour, heavy ....⅓ cup butter and ⅔ cup milk in any sour milk recipe
1 tsp Dried Herbs ....1 tbsp fresh herbs
1 cup Whole Milk ....½ cup evaporated milk and ½ cup water
....or 1 cup reconstituted nonfat dry milk and 1 tbsp butter
1 package Active Dry Yeast ....1 cake compressed yeast
1 tbsp Instant Minced Onion, rehydrated ....1 small fresh onion
1 tbsp Prepared Mustard..1 tsp dry mustard
⅛ tsp Garlic Powder ....1 small pressed clove of garlic
1 lb Whole Dates...1½ cup pitted and cut dates
3 medium Bananas...1 cup mashed bananas
3 cups dry Corn Flakes..1 cup crushed corn flakes
10 miniature Marshmallows ....1 large marshmallow

✒ EGGPLANT DRESSING ✒

¼ CUP (63ML)	OLIVE OIL	4 CUPS (1 LITER)	EGGPLANT,
1 CUP (250ML)	ONION, CHOPPED		PEELED AND CUBED
1 TBSP (15ML)	GARLIC, MINCED	2 CUPS (500ML)	COOKED HAM
¼ CUP (63ML)	PARSLEY, DRIED	¼ TSP (1.25ML)	CAYENNE PEPPER
½ TSP (2.5ML)	SALT	4 CUPS (1 LITER)	ITALIAN BREAD CRUMBS
½ LB (225G)	SMALL SHRIMP, PEELED		

In a skillet heat oil on medium high heat, add onion, garlic, parsley, salt and shrimp. Cook on medium heat until shrimp turns pink. Reduce heat. Add eggplant and simmer until eggplant cooks down, about 20 minutes. Add ham and pepper and cook 5 more minutes stirring occasionally. Add 3 cups bread crumbs and simmer 3-5 minutes. Remove and put into a casserole dish and top with a layer of bread crumbs. Cook at 350°F (175°C) for 15 minutes with lid on. Remove lid, cook until brown on top. Serves 8-10.

∾ RED BEANS AND RICE ∾

1 LB (450G)	RED KIDNEY BEANS
3 QTS (3 LTR.)	WATER
2 CUPS (500ML)	ONIONS
1 CUP (250ML)	BELL PEPPER
½ CUP (125ML)	CELERY
2 TBSP (30ML)	GARLIC
1 TBSP (15ML)	PARSLEY
2 TBSP (30ML)	SALT
2 TBSP (30ML)	BLACK PEPPER
2 TBSP (30ML)	CHILI POWDER
2 LB (900G)	PICKLED PORK OR HAM CHUNKS
	BE SURE TO HAVE A BOTTLE OF
	TABASCO BRAND PEPPER SAUCE ON HAND

88

(CONTINUES)

Wash beans well then drain. In a 6 quart (6 liter) pot put beans and cover 3" (7.5cm) with water (about 3 qts. or ltrs.). Allow beans to soak for several hours if possible. Chop all vegetables to a fine consistency. After soaking heat beans on high heat until boiling. Take out ½ of beans and reserve. Add onions, bell pepper, celery, garlic and parsley. Stir well. Bring to a hard boil, reduce heat to maintain boil. Be sure to stir often and add water to maintain level as needed. Add salt, black pepper, chili powder, reserved beans and pickle pork or chunk ham and simmer boil for 2 hours. Serve over rice.

❧ Four Cheese Beef & Pork Lasagna ❧

1 LB (450G)	LASAGNA NOODLES
2 TBSP (30ML)	SALT
¾ LB (338G)	LEAN BEEF, GROUND
¾ LB (338G)	PORK, GROUND
3 TBSP (45ML)	OLIVE OIL
1 CUP (250ML)	ONION, CHOPPED MEDIUM
½ CUP (125ML)	BELL PEPPER, CHOPPED MEDIUM
¼ CUP (63ML)	CELERY, CHOPPED FINE
3 TBSP (45ML)	GARLIC, MINCED
3 TBSP (45ML)	PARSLEY FLAKES
3 TBSP (45ML)	WHOLE SWEET BASIL
1 TBSP (15ML)	WHOLE OREGANO
1 TBSP (15ML)	FENNEL SEED

(CONTINUES)

2 TSP (10ML)	CARAWAY SEED
1 TSP (5ML)	ANISE SEED
1 TBSP (15ML)	SALT
1 TBSP (15ML)	BLACK PEPPER
1 QUART (1 LITER)	CRUSHED PEELED TOMATO
1½ CUPS (375ML)	TOMATO PASTE
1 CUP (250ML)	CHICKEN STOCK
1 TBSP (15ML)	GRANULATED SUGAR
1 CUP (250ML)	PARMESAN CHEESE, GRATED
1 CUP (250ML)	ROMANO CHEESE, GRATED
2 CUPS (500ML)	RICOTTA CHEESE
1 LB (450ML)	MOZZARELLA CHEESE, SHREDDED
1 TSP (5ML)	ADDITIONAL WHOLE OREGANO
	PAN SPRAY

(CONTINUES)

In a 8 quart (8 liter) pot heat 6 quarts (6 liters) of water to boil. When water begins a rapid boil add 2 tbsp (30ml) salt and stir well. Water will return to a boil immediately. Add lasagna noodles one at a time until all are added. Slowly and gently push the noodles into the boiling water until completely submerged. Bring back to a boil, stir, cover and reduce heat to low.

Set timer to 12 minutes. Stir occasionally to assure separation of noodles. Check until noodles are al dante' or cooked firm. Immediately run cold water into pot until temperature is tepid. Reserve.

In a 6 quart (6 liter) pot brown ground beef and pork until brown. Remove all fat, return to high heat. Add olive oil and heat to hot. Add onion, bell pepper, celery, garlic, parsley, basil, oregano, fennel, caraway, anise, salt and pepper and simmer on high heat until onions begin to brown. Add crushed peeled tomato, stir well. Next slowly add tomato paste and blend in until all is added. Add chicken stock and stir well. Bring to a rolling boil, reduce heat and stir well (be sure to scrape the bottom of the pot and blend it in well). Add sugar and stir in well. Cover and reduce heat to very low. Simmer for 45 minutes stirring frequently. Reserve for assembly.

(CONTINUES)

To assemble, spray the bottom of a 13" x 9" x 2" (33 x 23 x 5cm) baking pan. Reserve 2 cups of meat sauce for the top. Next, put a layer (about ⅓" of remaining meat sauce in the bottom of the pan and spread evenly. Sprinkle with parmesan, romano and small clumps of ricotta cheeses. Put a layer of overlapped lasagna noodles on top of meat sauce. Continue process until there is a thin layer of meat sauce on top. Sprinkle shredded mozzarella cheese and oregano on top. Cover with a strip of aluminum foil (Note: if you spray the inside of the foil before covering it will not stick to the cheese when you remove it). Cut and serve.

∽ Cooked Rice ∾

It seems to be one of the most asked questions. Everywhere I go someone will eventually ask me how I cook my rice. I have heard some of the most cockeyed methods of getting the "perfect rice". What I have to say about that is if the way you cook your rice is working for you and it is different from the way I do it, then more power to ya. If you are looking for a way to improve the pasty mess you have been serving your family then believe me this recipe will be a revelation. Don't make a big deal out of it.

The first suggestion I have for you is to use a long grain rice. A converted or par-boiled rice is even better for beautiful separate rice. The second suggestion is to learn a simple formula for determining the amount of water used in the cooking process; which is for every cup of rice, you add 2 cups of water, (or for healthier rice add a cup of stock). Always salt to taste and always cook it the same way. Which brings me to my third suggestion. Bring water (or stock)

(Continues)

to a boil and add the proper amount of rice (½ of the amount of liquid). Add salt, a little oil or butter, bring back to a boil, cover, reduce heat to very low and simmer for exactly 20 minutes. If you do this you will have perfect rice every time.

SUGGESTED RECIPE FOR 6 CUPS OF COOKED RICE

4 CUPS (1 LITER)	WATER OR STOCK
2 TSP (10ML)	SALT
2 CUPS (500ML)	LONG GRAIN OR CONVERTED RICE, UNCOOKED

Heat water or stock to boiling. Add salt and stir. Add rice and stir well. Bring back to boil, stir, cover, reduce heat to lowest setting and cook undisturbed for 20 minutes. Remove from heat, uncover and serve.

‷ DIRTY RICE ‷

¾ LB (338G)	BEEF, GROUND	6 CUPS (1.5 LITERS)	CHICKEN STOCK
¾ LB (338G)	PORK, GROUND	1 TBSP (15ML)	CAYENNE PEPPER
¼ LB (113G)	CHICKEN LIVERS, GROUND	1 TBSP (15ML)	SALT
¼ LB (113G)	CHICKEN GIZZARDS, GROUND	1 TBSP (15ML)	PAPRIKA
		10 DROPS	TABASCO BRAND PEPPER SAUCE
2 CUPS (500ML)	ONION		
1 CUP (250ML)	GREEN PEPPER	3 CUPS (750ML)	LONG GRAIN OR CONVERTED RICE, UNCOOKED
½ CUP (125ML)	CELERY		
¼ CUP (63ML)	FRESH PARSLEY	2 CUPS (500ML)	GREEN ONION, CHOPPED
3 TBSP (45ML)	GARLIC		

(CONTINUES)

In a 6 quart (6 liter) pot brown ground beef and ground pork. Add ground chicken livers and gizzards and brown, stirring occasionally until all meat is completely brown and broken fine. In a food processor, process all onion, green pepper, celery, parsley and garlic to very fine. Add it to the pot and stir well. Simmer for 10 minutes. Add chicken stock and bring to a boil. Reduce heat to low simmer and allow oil to rise to the top. Skim off all the oil and return to high heat.

Next, add cayenne, salt, paprika and TABASCO Brand Pepper Sauce and stir very well. Add rice and stir until well blended. Cover and reduce heat to very low. Set timer for 20 minutes and simmer until timer goes off. Remove from heat and add chopped green onion. Mix well and serve in a bowl.

OPTION: Instead of adding 4 cups (1 liter) of chicken stock to the mixture you can add ½ cup (125ml) and simmer until moisture is gone and then add the mixture to cooked rice. Blend the mixture as you like it. Be sure to garnish with chopped green onion.

❧ PECAN RICE ❧

¼ LB (113G)	BUTTER	2 TBSP (30ML)	FRESH PARSLEY, CHOPPED
1 CUP (250ML)	ONION, CHOPPED COARSE	2 TBSP (30ML)	FRESH BASIL, CHOPPED
½ CUP (125ML)	RED BELL PEPPER, CUT IN STRIPS	1 TSP (5ML)	SALT
		1 TSP (5ML)	BLACK PEPPER
¼ CUP (63ML)	GREEN BELL PEPPER, CUT IN STRIPS	5 DASHES	TABASCO BRAND PEPPER SAUCE
¼ CUP (63ML)	YELLOW BELL PEPPER, CUT IN STRIPS	1 CUP (250ML)	PECAN HALVES, PEELED
		3 CUPS (750ML)	RICE, COOKED
2 TBSP (30ML)	GARLIC, MINCED	¼ CUP (63ML)	GREEN ONION, CHOPPED

(CONTINUES)

In a 3 quart (3 liter) saucepan heat butter on high heat until melted. Immediately add onion, all bell pepper, garlic, parsley and basil and saute' until onion begins to brown. Next, add salt, pepper, TABASCO and pecan halves and stir well. Saute' for 5 minutes, then add cooked rice and mix in well, keeping on high heat until completely mixed. Remove from heat and add chopped green onion over the top to garnish. Serve.

⌘ POTATOES AU GRATIN ⌘

4 LB (1 KG+800G)	LARGE RUSSET POTATOES
¼ LB (113G)	BUTTER
2 TBSP (30ML)	ALL-PURPOSE FLOUR
2 TSP (10ML)	SALT
2 TSP (10ML)	BLACK PEPPER
3 CUPS (750ML)	HEAVY CREAM
8 OZ (225G)	CREAM CHEESE
8 OZ (225G)	SHARP CHEDDAR CHEESE, GRATED
8 OZ (225G)	AMERICAN CHEESE

(CONTINUES)

Peel potatoes and cut into ¼" (6 mm) slices then rinse. Put potatoes into a 6 quart (6 liter) pot and cover with water. Put on high heat and set timer for 20 minutes. When timer goes off potatoes should be 80% cooked. Drain and put into an ample casserole dish.

Meanwhile, in a 2 quart (2 liter) saucepan melt butter and add flour, salt and pepper. Whisk together and continue until mixture becomes bubbly. Slowly add heavy cream, whisking constantly until all is added. Break up the cream cheese and add in small chunks until all is added and whisk until totally blended. Next, add 6 ounces (168g) each of sharp cheddar and american cheeses. Continue to whisk until totally blended. Pre-heat oven to 350°F (175°C). Pour over the potatoes in the casserole and carefully mix in well. Sprinkle remaining cheese over the top of the mixture, cover and place in the oven for 25 minutes. If you want the top cheese to be slightly browned then remove the lid and put back into the oven for another 5 minutes or until desired color. Serve.

ᴓ LYONNAISE POTATOES ᴓ

4 LB (1KG+800G)	RUSSET POTATOES
¼ LB (113G)	BUTTER
3	LARGE ONIONS, CUT INTO ¼" (6MM) SLICES
2 TSP (10ML)	SALT
2 TSP (10ML)	BLACK PEPPER
½ CUP (125ML)	EVAPORATED MILK

Put potatoes into a large enough pot to cover with water by 2" (5cm). Leave peeling on. After about 25 minutes begin to check the potatoes with a knife. When the knife goes through the potato easily, they are done.

(CONTINUES)

Meanwhile, in a large skillet melt butter then add peeled and sliced onions and saute' until onions are beginning to brown and all moisture is gone from the skillet. Remove from heat and reserve in the skillet.

When potatoes are done, drain and peel (Note: They will peel easily with a paring knife. They will be hot, so use a pot holder or towel to hold while peeling). As you complete the peeling process cut the potato into several pieces and put back into the pot. When all potatoes are peeled and placed back into the pot return onions to high heat. Place potatoes on medium heat, add salt, pepper and evaporated milk. Stir gently to slightly break up potatoes and to heat milk. When onion mixture is very hot remove from heat and add to the potato mixture. Remove potato mixture from heat and whip the potatoes and onion mixture to desired texture. You may add more milk if you desire. Serve.

✎ New Orleans Po-Boy Style French Bread ✎

3-3½ cups (750ml-825ml)	Bread Flour, can use All-purpose Flour	1½ cups (375ml)	Very Warm Water, 110-115°F (44-47°C)
1 tbsp (15ml)	Vinegar	1 tbsp (15ml)	Dry Yeast
1½ tsp (7.5ml)	Salt	¼ cup (63ml)	Vegetable Oil
1½ tsp (7.5ml)	Sugar	¼ cup (56g)	Butter

In a food processor fitted with blade attachment, pour 3 cups flour, vinegar and salt. Blend for five seconds to mix. In a large cup add sugar to warm water and stir, then add in yeast and mix until completely dissolved. Turn food processor on and slowly add yeast mixture to flour mixture until all has been added and blend until dough consistency is equal (10 seconds). If dough is not stiff enough, add flour a little at a time until dough is thick enough to handle. Grease a large bowl with oil, making sure both of your hands are greased as well. Pour dough into bowl and coat with remaining oil turning over the dough until it is

(Continues)

completely coated with oil. Let rise in a warm place, covered, for about 1 to 1½ hours, or until dough about doubles in size. Punch down the dough until all air is out, then divide dough in half and place in a two sided french bread pan that has been greased. The dough will seem limp, so you do not have to shape, other than to even the dough end to end. Let rise in a warm place until doubled (about one hour). Place oven rack in center of oven and pre-heat to 400°F (205°C). When dough rises, brush lightly but generously with melted butter and place on center rack in oven and bake for 45 minutes or until the top is golden. Turn loaves over and bake 5-10 minutes more to brown bottom.

Slice and butter to eat. (It will be good enough to eat without butter). Makes great sandwich. If the bread survives long enough to get stale then process in a food processor to make great bread crumbs.

_____

_____

_____

_____

_____

_____

_____

_____

⧼ NOTES ⧽

∽ Seafood Section ∾

❧ Contents of Cans ❧

Size:	Average Contents
8-oz.	1 cup
Picnic	1¼ cups
No. 300	1¾ cups
No. 1 tall	2 cups
No. 303	2 cups
No. 2	2½ cups
No. 2½	3½ cups
No. 3	4 cups
No. 10	12 to 13 cups

Of the different sizes of cans used by commercial canners, these are the most common.

❧ General Oven Chart ❧

Very slow oven	250° to 300°F
Slow Oven	300° to 325°F
Moderate Oven	325° to 375°F
Medium Hot Oven	375° to 400°F
Hot Oven	400° to 450°F
Very Hot Oven	450° to 500°F

✇ STUFFED FLOUNDER ✇

2 MEDIUM	FLOUNDERS, 2-3 POUNDS (900G TO 1450G)
1 CUP (250ML)	ONION, FINELY CHOPPED
¼ CUP (63ML)	GREEN ONION, FINELY CHOPPED
½ CUP (125ML)	CELERY, FINELY CHOPPED
1 TSP (5ML)	SALT
1 TSP (5ML)	BLACK PEPPER
¼ CUP (63ML)	PARSLEY FLAKES
1 TBSP (15ML)	GARLIC, MINCED
1 TBSP (15ML)	CREOLE SEASONING, SEE SEASONING SECTION
1 LB (450G)	LUMP CRAB MEAT, CHECK FOR SHELL
¾ CUP (175ML)	ITALIAN BREAD CRUMBS
1½ CUPS (375ML)	SHREDDED MOZZARELLA CHEESE, OPTIONAL
1	LEMON

(CONTINUES)

Clean and debone flounder*. Cut a slit in the top during deboning. In a heavy skillet melt butter and add onion, green onion, celery, salt, pepper, parsley and garlic. Simmer 4-5 minutes on medium heat. Add creole seasoning and crab meat and mix well. Add bread crumbs and cook. You may need to add a slight bit of water to achieve consistency, a slightly dry mixture is best. Remove and let cool. In a bowl combine mixture with cheese, if desired and stuff flounder.

In a preheated 350°F (175°C) oven bake for 20-25 minutes covered and then uncover and bake another 5 minutes. Squeeze lemon on top of flounder and serve. To eat just peel top skin away with your fork until you reach the finned part of the fish. Then pull the finned part away from the fish and remove. The small remaining bone at the end of the finned part will be removed with the fin. Then dig in! Serves 2.

*To debone the flounder and clean all you do is cut off the head just behind the dorsal fin. You will see the small gut area at the bottom of the fish. On an angle, cut the gut area totally

(CONTINUES)

off the fish (which will be a very small section at the bottom). The next step is to slide a very sharp boning knife along the top of the fish from the tail to the dorsal fin area that you just cut off. It should be right down the middle of the fish. Next you will slice the top meat away from the bone as you peel the meat away. When you reach the finned area stop and do the other side.

Next you will slide the knife just under the bones until you reach the finned area as well, making sure you cut all meat away from the front of the fish to the tail. The next step is to use a utility scissors to cut the bone along the fin area from the front to the tail. Crack the main vertebrae at the tail and remove the bone totally.

If this seems too difficult to do then just leave in the bone and peel the meat away as you eat the fish, and after the top is eaten the bottom meat will pull away from the bone like butter.

❧ Blackened Redfish ❧

To cook Blackened Redfish, there are some things you must know before you start.
First: If redfish is not available, select fish with a firm texture. Grouper or tuna for example.
Second: I recommend that you use a cast iron skillet to prepare this recipe because of the high heat and potential scorching from the preparation of this dish.
Third: Cook this outside on a grill that can give a high flame. Be prepared for smoking and possible burning of butter. Keep a lid ready to cover pan and put out any flame. It won't be that bad, but it is something that can happen. Don't panic and don't let this keep you from preparing this great New Orleans dish.

1 TBSP (15ML)	CAYENNE PEPPER	1 TBSP (15ML)	BLACK PEPPER
2 TBSP (30ML)	OREGANO	6	REDFISH FILETS, SKINNED
2 TBSP (30ML)	WHOLE DRIED THYME	2	LEMONS
1 TSP (5ML)	SALT	9 TBSP (252G)	BUTTER

(CONTINUES)

Combine cayenne, oregano, thyme, salt and black pepper and mix well. (If possible, crush to a powder). Lay fish out and sprinkle mixture over both sides. If fish is freshly thawed the natural moisture should be sufficient to hold spices to fish. If the fish is dry you may mist with water or squeeze lemon on fish before sprinkling seasoning.

Then in a cast iron skillet melt 1 tbsp (15ml) of butter (for each filet), on high heat. Place filets in butter. Squeeze lemon juice over fish. Notice that the fish will cook very fast. Resist turning over or removing from pan until the fish begins to blacken.

After cooking fish drain skillet and remove burnt pieces from pan. Drop remaining butter, lemon and spices into skillet and cook together over same high heat, stirring constantly until seasoning blackens. Pour over fish and serve.

Speckled Trout Almandine

1 CUP (250ML)	ALL-PURPOSE FLOUR
1 CUP (250ML)	CORN FLOUR OR SEASONED FISH FRY
1 TBSP (15ML)	CAYENNE PEPPER
1 TSP (5ML)	SALT
½ CUP (125ML)	FRESH PARSLEY, CHOPPED FINE
1	EGG
½ CUP (125ML)	HEAVY CREAM
1 TSP (5ML)	TABASCO BRAND PEPPER SAUCE
2 TBSP (30ML)	WORCESTERSHIRE SAUCE
1 CUP (250ML)	SLIVERED ALMOND PIECES
6 LARGE	TROUT FILETS, SKINNED
1 CUP (250ML)	OIL FOR FRYING

(CONTINUES)

In a bowl mix flour, corn flour or fish fry, cayenne pepper, salt and parsley. Mix well. Measure off ½ of mixture into a bowl. Add egg, cream, TABASCO Brand Pepper Sauce, worcestershire and mix well. In another bowl mix almond pieces with remaining flour mixture. Dip trout filets into wet mixture coating both sides thoroughly. Next dip coated trout into the dry mixture, containing almonds and coat thoroughly. In pre-heated oil fry fish on both sides until golden brown, about 3-5 minutes per side. Serve.

❧ STUFFED SHRIMP, BROILED OR FRIED ❧

¼ LB (113G)	BUTTER	2 TBSP (30ML)	LEMON JUICE
½ CUP (125ML)	GREEN ONION, FINELY MINCED	½ CUP (125ML)	WATER
1½ CUPS (375ML)	ONION, FINELY MINCED	18-24	LARGE SHRIMP, PEEL EXCEPT FOR THE VERY END OF THE TAIL, BUTTERFLY, DEVEIN AND CLEAN
¼ CUP (63ML)	PARSLEY FLAKES		
2 TBSP (30ML)	GARLIC, CRUSHED		
1 TBSP (15ML)	CAYENNE PEPPER	3 CUPS (750ML)	OIL FOR FRYING OPTION
1 TSP (5ML)	SALT		
1 TSP (5ML)	DRIED WHOLE OREGANO, CRUSHED	1 CUP (250ML)	ITALIAN SEASONED BREAD CRUMBS
2 CUPS (500ML)	UNSALTED CRACKERS, CRUSHED FINE		

114

(CONTINUES)

In a 1 quart (1 liter) pot melt butter then add green onion, onion, parsley, garlic, cayenne, salt and oregano. Cook for 10-12 minutes on medium heat stirring 2-3 times. Add crackers, lemon juice and water. Cook another 10-12 minutes until mixture has thickened enough to pat into a ball. When mixture cools enough to handle pat around shrimp until a ball forms around the entire shrimp except for the tail. Place in broiling pan and broil with door open until brown. (Note: Keep some oil on the pan to prevent sticking).

Fry option: Heat to hot 3 cups oil in a saucepan. Put 1 cup Italian seasoned bread crumbs in a bowl. Roll stuffed shrimp in bread crumbs until completely coated. Place stuffed shrimp in oil and fry on a slightly reduced heat until browned.

❧ Hot and Spicy Baked Redfish Filet ❧

2 LARGE	REDFISH FILETS
1 TBSP (15ML)	CREOLE SEASONING, SEE SEASONING SECTION
2 TBSP (30ML)	BUTTER
1 TBSP (15ML)	LEMON JUICE
¼ CUP (63ML)	PICKAPEPPER SAUCE
1 CUP (250ML)	GREEN ONION, FINELY CHOPPED
½ CUP (125ML)	FRESH PARSLEY, FINELY CHOPPED

Generously sprinkle filet of fish with creole seasoning. Combine butter and lemon juice and pour over fish. Liberally brush on pickapepper sauce over fish. Place chopped green onion and parsley around fish. Bake at 400°F (205°C) for 20 minutes on bottom shelf. Serves 2.

✒ CAJUN SHRIMP CREOLE ✑

¼ CUP (63ML)	OLIVE OIL	1 TSP (5ML)	CAYENNE PEPPER,
2 TBSP (30ML)	ALL-PURPOSE FLOUR		ADJUST TO TASTE
1 CUP (250ML)	ONION, CHOPPED MEDIUM	¼ TSP (1.5ML)	BLACK PEPPER
½ CUP (125ML)	BELL PEPPER,	½ TSP (2.6ML)	SALT
	CHOPPED MEDIUM	2 CUPS (500ML)	SHRIMP, CLEANED & DEVEINED
2 TBSP (30ML)	GARLIC, MINCED	¼ CUP (63ML)	TOMATO PASTE
½ CUP (125ML)	PARSLEY FLAKES,	1 CUP (250ML)	TOMATO SAUCE
	DOUBLE IF FRESH	1 CUP (250ML)	WATER

In a 10" (25cm) skillet heat oil. Add flour, stir on medium heat until flour begins to brown. Add onion, bell pepper, garlic, parsley, cayenne, black pepper and salt. Simmer on medium heat until onion is limp and clear. Add shrimp, cook until all shrimp are pink. Add tomato paste, tomato sauce and water. Simmer 20 minutes on low heat. Serve over rice. Serves 3-4.

ᨔᨔ New Orleans Barbecue Shrimp ᨔᨔ

2 LB (900G)	SHRIMP, RINSED AND UNPEELED WITH HEADS ON
4	BAY LEAVES, CRUSHED FINE
1 TBSP (15ML)	BLACK PEPPER
2 TSP (10ML)	SALT
1 TBSP (15ML)	CAYENNE PEPPER
½ LB (225G)	BUTTER
½ CUP (125ML)	OLIVE OIL
2 TBSP (30ML)	CREOLE SEASONING, SEE SEASONING SECTION
4 CLOVES	GARLIC, MINCED
4 TSP (40ML)	DRIED ROSEMARY LEAVES, CRUSHED
½ CUP (125ML)	LEMON JUICE

Place shrimp in a large pan no more than two layers high. Sprinkle bay leaves under the layers of shrimp. Sprinkle pepper and salt to taste. Add cayenne and mix well. Melt butter in pot, add olive oil, creole seasoning, garlic, rosemary leaves and lemon juice. Mix well and pour over shrimp. Bake in oven at 350°F (175°C) about 30 minutes. Let cool, peel shrimp and eat as you peel. You can (I highly recommend) dip French bread in the butter sauce. See New Orleans style French bread recipe, page 104.

∽ SHRIMP ETOUFFEE ∾

¼ LB (113G)	BUTTER	1 TBSP (15ML)	CREOLE SEASONING,
1 CUP (250ML)	ONION, CHOPPED MEDIUM		SEE SEASONING SECTION
½ CUP (125ML)	BELL PEPPER,	1 TSP (5ML)	SALT
	CHOPPED MEDIUM	2 TSP (10ML)	BLACK PEPPER
¼ CUP (63ML)	CELERY, CHOPPED MEDIUM	1 TBSP (15ML)	TURMERIC
2 TBSP (30ML)	GARLIC, MINCED	1LB (450G)	SHRIMP, PEELED AND
2 TBSP (30ML)	PARSLEY FLAKES		DEVEINED
2 TBSP (30ML)	ALL-PURPOSE FLOUR		ADDITIONAL WATER TO
2 CUPS (500ML)	SEAFOOD STOCK OR WATER		ACHIEVE DESIRE TEXTURE
1¼ CUPS (313ML)	CREAM OF MUSHROOM SOUP		COOKED RICE

(CONTINUES)

In a 12" (30cm) skillet melt butter on high heat. Add onion, bell pepper, celery, garlic and parsley and saute' until onions begin to clear. Add flour and whisk until flour begins to brown. Add seafood stock, or water a little at a time whisking until all is blended. Mixture will begin to thicken slightly. Add cream of mushroom soup and stir in well. Add creole seasoning, salt, black pepper, turmeric and shrimp. Stir in well. If you need to adjust the texture thinner, then add water a little at a time making sure it is blended completely before adding more. Serve over cooked rice. Serves 4-6.

⌾ SHRIMP & EGGPLANT REMY ⌾

1 LARGE	EGGPLANT, ABOUT 4 HEAPING CUPS (1 LITER)	1 TSP (5ML)	SALT
		1 TBSP (15ML)	CRUSHED ROSEMARY
1 TBSP (15ML)	SALT	1 TBSP (15ML)	WHOLE SWEET BASIL
½ CUP (125ML)	OLIVE OIL, EXTRA VIRGIN	1 TBSP (15ML)	PARSLEY FLAKES
1 CUP (250ML)	ONION, CHOPPED MEDIUM	1 TSP (5ML)	WHOLE THYME
½ CUP (125ML)	SHALLOT, CHOPPED FINE	6 DROPS	TABASCO BRAND PEPPER SAUCE
¼ CUP (63ML)	GREEN ONION, CHOPPED FINE		
		¼ CUP (63ML)	FINE BRANDY
3 TBSP (45ML)	GARLIC, MINCED		COOKED FETTUCCINE
¼ CUP (63ML)	WATER		FRESH PARMESAN CHEESE, GRATED
1 LB (450G)	SHRIMP, LARGE PEELED, BUTTERFLIED & DEVEINED		
		¼ CUP (63ML)	GREEN ONION, CHOPPED

(CONTINUES)

Peel, cut and cube eggplant. Place in a pot large enough to hold covered with water. Add 1 tbsp (15ml) salt and place on high heat until boiling. Reduce heat to simmer and cook another 15 minutes. Drain and reserve.

In a 4 quart (4 liter) pot on high heat, heat olive oil to hot. Add onion, shallot, green onion and garlic and stir well. Simmer for 3 minutes. Add reserved eggplant and stir well. Add water and stir. Bring to bubble, reduce heat, cover and simmer for 10 minutes, do not stir. Uncover, return to high heat, stir and continue for 5 minutes. Add shrimp and stir in well. When moisture is gone add salt, rosemary, basil, parsley and whole thyme. Stir well. Keep on high heat until mixture just begins to stick to the bottom. Add TABASCO and brandy. Stir well. Allow just a little brandy to spill into the fire to set the brandy in the pot on fire. Remove from heat and allow fire to go out on its own. Stir well, cover and let stand for 5 minutes. Serve over fettuccine. Parmesan cheese and fresh green onion goes well on top. Serves 4-6.

∞ Oysters/Bienville ∞

2 DOZ	OYSTERS, IN SHELLS	1 TSP (5ML)	BLACK PEPPER
¼ CUP (57G)	BUTTER	½ TSP (2.5ML)	CAYENNE PEPPER
¼ CUP (63ML)	GREEN ONION, MINCED	2	EGG YOLKS
1 TBSP (15ML)	GARLIC, MINCED	TOPPING:	
¼ CUP (63ML)	FRESH PARSLEY, CHOPPED FINE	½ CUP (125ML)	PARMESAN CHEESE
½ LB (225G)	SHRIMP, COOKED AND MINCED	¼ CUP (63ML)	ITALIAN SEASONED BREAD CRUMBS
¼ CUP (63ML)	ALL-PURPOSE FLOUR	¼ TSP (1.3ML)	SALT, OPTIONAL; CONSIDER SALTINESS OF OYSTERS AND PARMESAN CHEESE
1 CUP (250ML)	HEAVY CREAM		
1 CUP (250ML)	WHITE WINE		JUICE FROM 2 LEMONS

(CONTINUES)

First you must open or shuck the oysters. If you don't have an oyster knife then it is easy to open commercially cultivated oysters with a common can opener. Some call them church keys.

Locate the hinge of the oyster. It will appear as an overlapping end of the oyster. Place the pointed end of the can opener in the hinge as far as possible and pry to break the hinge. When oyster opens you need to stick a knife along the flat shell side of the oyster until you cut the top muscle. The top shell will fall off (Note: the flattest side of the oyster is the top). Carefully cut the bottom muscle of the oyster to free the oyster from the shell. Save the bottom curved part of the oyster shell to be well cleaned and scrubbed to remove soil and any shell pieces. Save the oysters in their juice.

Next, in a heavy skillet melt butter on medium heat. Add green onion, garlic, parsley and shrimp and simmer 8-10 minutes. The shrimp will release additional moisture so simmer until most of the liquid evaporates. Add flour and stir until well blended. Cook for 3 more minutes stirring constantly.

(CONTINUES)

Next, stir in heavy cream until combined. Add white wine, pepper, cayenne and bring to a bubble. Remove from heat and slowly add egg yolks and whisk until completely blended. Let cool.

THE ASSEMBLY:

In a separate bowl combine cheese and breadcrumbs and mix well. Clean oysters well and dry them by placing on a paper towel. Then place oysters on a shell and place on a rack or in a baking pan filled with rock salt. Top each oyster with shrimp mixture then sprinkle with cheese and bread crumb mixture. Squeeze lemon over all 24 oysters and bake in a 400-425°F (205-220°C) pre-heated oven for 10-15 minutes until brown and bubbly.

CREOLE/CAJUN SEASONING

❧ Equivalent Chart ❧

3 TSP	1 TBSP
2 TBSP	⅛ CUP
4 TBSP	¼ CUP
8 TBSP	½ CUP
16 TBSP	1 CUP
5 TBSP + 1 TSP	⅓ CUP
12 TBSP	¾ CUP
4 OZ	½ CUP
8 OZ	1 CUP
16 OZ	1 LB
1 OZ	2 TBSP, FAT OR LIQUID
2 CUP	1 PINT
2 PINT	1 QUART
1 QUART	4 CUP
⅝ CUP	½ CUP + 2 TBSP
⅞ CUP	¾ CUP + 2 TBSP
1 JIGGER	1½ FL. OZ. (3 TBSP)
8 TO 10 EGG WHITES	1 CUP
12 TO 14 EGG YOLKS	1 CUP
1 CUP UNWHIPPED CREAM	2 CUP WHIPPED CREAM
1 LB. SHREDDED AMERICAN CHEESE	4 CUPS
¼ LB. CRUMBLED BLEU CHEESE	1 CUP
1 LEMON	3 TBSP JUICE
1 ORANGE	⅓ CUP JUICE
1 LB UNSHELLED WALNUTS	1½ TO 1¾ CUP SHELLED
2 CUPS FAT	1 LB
1 LB. BUTTER	2 CUPS OR 4 STICKS
2 CUPS GRANULATED SUGAR	1 LB
3½-4 CUPS UNSIFTED POWDERED SUGAR	1 LB
2¼ CUPS PACKED BROWN SUGAR	1 LB
4 CUPS SIFTED FLOUR	1 LB
4½ CUPS CAKE FLOUR	1 LB
3½ CUPS UNSIFTED WHOLE WHEAT FLOUR	1 LB
4 OZ. (1-1¼ CUPS) UNCOOKED MACARONI	2¼ CUP COOKED
7 OZ. SPAGHETTI	4 CUP COOKED
4 OZ. (1½ TO 2 CUPS) UNCOOKED NOODLES	2 CUPS COOKED
28 SALTINE CRACKERS	1 CUP CRUMBS
4 SLICES BREAD	1 CUP CRUMBS
14 SQUARE GRAHAM CRACKERS	1 CUP CRUMBS
22 VANILLA WAFERS	1 CUP CRUMBS

THIS CREOLE/CAJUN SEASONING SECTION is designed to help you to blend your own Creole/Cajun seasonings. You are free to experiment with the different blends to satisfy your own taste. In fact, there is a guideline for your own blend of seasoning later in this section. You will certainly find many different blends of Creole/Cajun seasoning on the market. In fact no two blends are the same. Seasoning blends are basically the tastes of the blender. There is no right or wrong in blending seasonings. What really matters is the blend that works for you. This book offers my blends, (or at least one version of each recipe) for your discretion. All these blends are tried and proven to provide a consistent way to season your food the "New Orleans" way. It will also serve to improve your knowledge of cooking New Orleans style.

CREOLE/CAJUN SEASONING

USE ONLY DRIED SEASONINGS

1 CUP (250ML)	SALT	½ CUP (125ML)	GRANULATED GARLIC
2 TBSP (30ML)	CAYENNE PEPPER	¼ CUP (63ML)	ONION POWDER
¼ CUP (63ML)	BLACK PEPPER	1½ TBSP (23ML)	CELERY SEED

In a food processor add salt and cayenne pepper. Process for 30 seconds. Add black pepper, granulated garlic and process another 15 seconds. Add remaining ingredients and process another minute. Store in air-tight container. Use for gumbo, jambalaya, etouffee or for your regular cooking. You can also use like salt at the dinner table. Makes about 2¼ cups (563ml).

CREOLE SEAFOOD SEASONING

USE ONLY DRIED SEASONINGS

1 CUP (250ML)	SALT	¼ CUP (63ML)	GRANULATED GARLIC
½ CUP (125ML)	WHOLE SWEET BASIL	½ CUP (125ML)	ONION POWDER
2 TBSP (30ML)	CAYENNE PEPPER	¼ CUP (63ML)	WHOLE THYME
¼ CUP (63ML)	BLACK PEPPER		

In a food processor add salt and whole sweet basil. Blend until color is evenly distributed. Next, add granulated garlic and cayenne pepper. Process another 30 seconds. Add remaining ingredients and blend 1 minute. You can use this in all stages of cooking. Sprinkle on top of baked or broiled fish—use in pot cooking or use at the dinner table. Makes 3 cups (750ml) of seasoning.

✍ Creole/Cajun Vegetable Seasoning ✍

USE ONLY DRIED SEASONINGS

1 CUP (250ML)	SALT	½ CUP (125ML)	PARSLEY FLAKES
1 CUP (250ML)	WHITE PEPPER	1½ TBSP (23ML)	GARLIC POWDER
¼ CUP (63ML)	CAYENNE PEPPER	¼ CUP (63ML)	ONION POWDER
¼ CUP (63ML)	BLACK PEPPER	¼ CUP (63ML)	CURRY POWDER

Put all ingredients in a food processor and blend for 2 minutes. Use in cooking or at the dinner table. Good for all types of vegetables, especially steamed. Makes almost 3½ cups (837ml) seasoning.

∽ Blackened Seasoning for Chicken ∾

Use only Dried Seasonings

½ CUP (125ML)	CAYENNE PEPPER
1 CUP (250ML)	WHOLE OREGANO
½ CUP (125ML)	WHOLE THYME
¼ CUP (63ML)	SALT
½ CUP (125ML)	BLACK PEPPER
½ CUP (125ML)	PAPRIKA

In a food processor blend cayenne pepper, whole oregano and whole thyme for 1 minute. Next add salt, black pepper, paprika and blend for another minute. Blackened seasoning is used to coat the chicken and fry in very hot butter for a short period of time. Follow your recipe instructions. Use only in cooking. This is not a good table seasoning. Makes 3¼ cups (813ml) seasoning.

❧ Blackened Seasoning for Fish ❧

USE ONLY DRIED SEASONINGS

½ CUP (125ML)	CAYENNE PEPPER
1 CUP (250ML)	WHOLE OREGANO
½ CUP (125ML)	WHOLE THYME
1 TBSP (15ML)	SALT
1 TBSP (15ML)	BLACK PEPPER

In a food processor blend cayenne pepper, whole oregano and whole thyme for 1 minute. Next add salt, black pepper and process for another minute. Blackened seasoning is used to coat the fish and fry in very hot butter for a short period of time. Follow your recipe instructions. Use only in cooking. This is not a good table seasoning. Makes 2 cups + 2 tbsp (530ml) seasoning.

✺ BLACKENED SEASONING FOR BEEF ✺

USE ONLY DRIED SEASONINGS

½ CUP (125ML)	CAYENNE PEPPER
½ CUP (125ML)	WHOLE OREGANO
¼ CUP (63ML)	CRUSHED ROSEMARY
½ CUP (125ML)	PAPRIKA
¼ CUP (63ML)	SALT
¼ CUP (63ML)	BLACK PEPPER

In a food processor blend cayenne pepper, whole oregano and crushed rosemary for 1 minute. Next add paprika, salt, black pepper and process for another minute. Blackened seasoning is used to coat the meat and fry in very hot butter for a short period of time. Follow your recipe instructions. Use only in cooking. This is not a good table seasoning. Makes 2½ cups (625ml) seasoning.

✑ YOUR OWN BLEND OF SEASONING ✑

Making your own seasoning blend is really very simple if you give some thought to your cooking habits and techniques. First thing is to go to your seasoning rack or shelf and remove your most used seasonings. Next place the seasonings that you use in everything (or almost everything) on the side. If you think about it you will find that you use these seasonings in the same proportion in virtually everything you cook. Measure out the amounts of these seasonings as you normally use them. If you don't usually measure then you need to pay attention to the amounts of each seasoning that you use. Write it down each time you cook, and make sure that the ratio of seasonings is consistent each time you use them. Once you have established the seasonings you use–in the amounts and ratio you use them, you can begin to blend. Use the chart below to help you mix.

1 TSP (5ML)	X 3	=	1 TBSP (15ML)
1 TBSP (15ML)	X 4	=	¼ CUP (63ML)
¼ CUP (63ML)	X 4	=	1 CUP (250ML)
1 CUP (250ML)	X 4	=	1 QUART (1 LITER)

When you have established the proper ratios of dry seasonings that you use, it is easy to make your blend. In a food processor add all the ingredients in the proper amounts and blend for 1 to 2 minutes, or until you are satisfied that the blending is complete. When you use your dry seasoning blend be sure to compile the amount of each of the dry seasonings that you use in cooking. Add those amounts together and use that much of the blend.

(CONTINUES)

EXAMPLE: You have established the cooking ratios of your favorite dry seasonings to be the following:

1 TBSP (15ML)	SALT	1 TBSP (15ML)	ONION POWDER
1 TSP (5ML)	BACK PEPPER	2 TBSP (30ML)	PARSLEY FLAKES
1 TBSP (15ML)	GRANULATED GARLIC	2 TBSP (30ML)	WHOLE SWEET BASIL

Now that you know the amounts and ratios of the dry seasonings that you use most, you can make your blend. For this example, say you want to blend enough to make 10 average recipes. Then you simply multiply the ingredients times 10.

1 TBSP (15ML) SALT	X 10	=	10 TBSP (150ML)	=	½ CUP + 2 TBSP
1 TSP (5ML) BLACK PEPPER	X 10	=	10 TSP (50ML)	=	3 TBSP + 1 TSP
1 TBSP (15ML) GRANULATED GARLIC	X 10	=	10 TBSP (150ML)	=	½ CUP + 2 TBSP
1 TBSP (15ML) ONION POWDER	X 10	=	10 TBSP (150ML)	=	½ CUP + 2 TBSP
2 TBSP (30ML) PARSLEY FLAKES	X 10	=	20 TBSP (300ML)	=	1+¼ CUPS
2 TBSP (30ML) WHOLE SWEET BASIL	X 10	=	20 TBSP (300ML)	=	1+¼ CUPS

(CONTINUES)

Now that you know the proper amounts to blend, your recipe is as follows:

½ CUP + 2 TBSP (150ML)	SALT
3 TBSP + 1 TSP (50ML)	BLACK PEPPER
½ CUP + 2 TBSP (150ML)	GRANULATED GARLIC
½ CUP + 2 TBSP (150ML)	ONION POWDER
1+¼ CUPS (300ML)	PARSLEY FLAKES
1+¼ CUPS (300ML)	WHOLE SWEET BASIL

Place all ingredients in a food processor and blend for 1 to 2 minutes until all ingredients are totally blended. Note: the dry leafy ingredients will reduce in measurement by ½ when totally blended. When using the seasoning blend, take this into consideration.

(CONTINUES)

EXAMPLE: Your originally established example seasoning recipe.

1 TBSP (15ML)	SALT
1 TSP (5ML)	BLACK PEPPER
1 TBSP (15ML)	GRANULATED GARLIC
1 TBSP (15ML)	ONION POWDER
2 TBSP (30ML)	PARSLEY FLAKES (1 TBSP PROCESSED)
2 TBSP (30ML)	WHOLE SWEET BASIL (1 TBSP PROCESSED)

Add all ingredients to establish the total to use in each recipe. In this example the total is 5 tbsp + 1 tsp (80ml). (Remember that the dry leafy ingredients were cut by ½ to measure actual mass).

(CONTINUES)

Per Use Amount

5 TBSP + 1 TSP (80ML) = ¼ CUP + 1 TBSP + 1 TSP

Remember that recipes will call for different amounts of seasoning to accommodate different quantities of food cooked. When deciding how much to use in that recipe, adjust the amount of the blend you use by the amount of salt you use and that will give you the proper amount for all the other ingredients in the blend. For instance, if you would use 1 tbsp (15ml) salt then use the established per use amount. If you use 2 tbsp (30ml) of salt then double the established per use amount, etc.

Note: Don't forget to write the recipe for your blend down. File it where you can find it for future blending.

I suggest you use the next page entitled "NOTES" to keep you seasoning blend recipe stored.

∽ Soon to be Available ∾

"Cajun Talk"

A EXCITING NEW PERIODICAL CONTAINING
- Up-to-date Cajun Menus
- Louisiana Product Information
- Information on Local Attractions
  and Special Events in south Louisiana
- Articles about the People, Music, History
  and Lifestyles in south Louisiana
  ...and much more.

For more information, send your name and address to:
Remy Laterrade • P.O. Box 3942 • Lafayette, LA 70502-1943

✂ LOUISIANA PRODUCTS ✂

Wherever I go to demonstrate cooking I am constantly asked for information about ordering Louisiana products once the out of state (or country) buyer gets home. It also occurred to me that many people are receiving this book as a gift or are buying without meeting someone who can give information about Louisiana products to them. If you write to me and provide your mailing address, I will be happy to provide you with Louisiana businesses that carry meats, spices and gifts. The offering is adequate to provide you with sources of quality hard to get products out of our fair state.

If you have received this book as a gift, have ordered from me directly or you purchased this book out of Louisiana, and are having trouble getting the information that you want, then don't hesitate to write to me:

(CONTINUES)

Remy Laterrade
P.O. Box 3942
Lafayette, LA 70502-3942

If you haven't had a chance to visit Louisiana, then I invite you to enjoy our "food, folks and fun" as well as the finest place in the country for architecture and other great sights. The plantations, the theme parks, the music, food and culture are all here for you to come and enjoy. While you are making your plans to visit us, then please consider visiting Lafayette. We are located on I-10 exit #'s 100, 101 and 103.

YA'LL COME!

SHIP TO:
NAME

UPS ADDRESS

CITY_____STATE _____ZIP _____

MAILING ADDRESS

CITY_____STATE _____ZIP _____

PHONE

❏ PLEASE ADD MY NAME TO YOUR MAILING LIST

Make Checks Payable to:
Remy Laterrade • P.O. Box 3942 • Lafayette, LA 70502 • Do Not Send Cash!

'Dat Little Louisiana Plantation Cookbook by Remy, $4.95 plus S&H
'Dat Little New Orleans Creole Cookbook by Remy, $4.95 plus S&H
'Dat Little Cajun Cookbook by Remy, $4.95 plus S&H
I Want 'Dat Cajun Cookbook by Remy,
   First Copy, $12.95 plus S&H. Each additional copy $11.95 plus S&H

		Quantity	Total
I Want 'Dat Cajun Cookbook by Remy,	First Copy, $12.95	_____	_____
	Each Additional Copy, $11.95	_____	_____
'Dat Little New Orleans Creole Cookbook by Remy,	Each Copy, $4.95	_____	_____
'Dat Little Louisiana Plantation Cookbook by Remy,	Each Copy, $4.95	_____	_____
'Dat Little Cajun Cookbook by Remy,	Each Copy, $4.95	_____	_____
Shipping and Handling,	First Book, $2.50		_____
Shipping and Handling,	Each Additional Book, $1.50	_____	_____
		Total	_____